BEYOND
HALF

Practical Wisdom for Your Second Half

TIME®

Also by Bob Buford

Halftime: Moving from Success to Significance

Stuck in Halftime: Reinvesting Your One and Only Life

*Game Plan: Winning Strategies for the Second Half
of Your Life*

Finish Well: What People Who Really Live Do Differently

BEYOND
HALF
Practical Wisdom for Your Second Half
TIME®

BOB BUFORD

ZONDERVAN®
.com

ZONDERVAN

Beyond Halftime
Copyright © 2008 by The Leadership Network, Inc.

Requests for information should be addressed to:
Zondervan, 3900 Sparks Dr. SE, Grand Rapids, Michigan 49546

This edition: ISBN 978-0-310-34673-9 (softcover)

Library of Congress Cataloging-in-Publication Data

Buford, Bob.
    Beyond halftime : practical wisdom for your second half /
Bob Buford.
        p. cm.
    Companion to: Halftime.
    ISBN 978-0-310-28423-9 (hardcover)
    1. Middle-aged persons—Religious life. 2. Self-realization—Religious
aspects—Christianity. 3. Christian life. I. Title.
BV4579.5.B828 2009
248.8'4—dc22   2008046705

Interior design: Beth Shagene

First printing January 2016 / Printed in the United States of America

To those great souls
who join me on the journey
from success to significance

Contents

Introduction

Ever since the first edition of *Halftime* was published in 1995, I have had the privilege of hearing from hundreds of men and women who have decided to embark on the journey to significance. Hardly a week goes by without someone writing or emailing me to share a personal story and maybe ask a question or two. What began as an attempt to tell my own story of shifting my focus from success in my business to finding a way to use what I believe and what I have been given for a higher calling has all the markings of a genuine "movement." Literally thousands of people who have also discovered that life is more than gaining and accumulating are now actively making their own corner of the world a brighter place. Sensing that this is bigger than anything I could have imagined, I created a website (www.activeenergy.net) to coach fellow "halftimers" and direct them to resources that will help them on their journey.

One of the resources that generates remarkable comment is a regular column I write for my website. It's called "Musings," and that's exactly what it is: ideas, thoughts, stories, and prayers that have helped me along the way and that somehow connect with those who have decided to really live out their beliefs. The popularity of these occasional musings on my website convinced me that people want to learn more about this phenomenon called halftime and provided the inspiration for this book. I have always said that you cannot travel this journey alone, thus I have prepared *Personal Coaching for Your Halftime Journey*. Although it is no substitute for a team of close friends — including your spouse — to accompany you along the way, this book is designed to provide you with inspiration and encouragement from someone who has now been in the second half for twenty-five years and can honestly say each year is better than the previous one.

In terms of length, this book is what I call a "flight book." You could easily read it from wheels up to touchdown on your next business trip. However, the purpose of my musings is to slow you down and get you to think more deeply about the challenges and opportunities that will come as you attempt to escape the gravity of the ordinary. The people who have the most difficult time reordering their lives based on the principles in *Halftime* are the ones who, in my opinion, are looking for a quick fix. It's ingrained in all of us, but especially in successful people. We have been hard-chargers, "get me to the bottom line" soldiers, for so long that words like *introspection*, *stillness*, and *listening* seem like barriers to get past rather than life rings to grasp and hold on to. So don't look at this book as another accomplishment to check off but as a companion to nudge you, maybe to provoke you, but especially to engage you. Read one chapter each day — or each week.

Take the time to wrestle with the questions and comments at the end of each chapter. If you have read *Halftime*, you know how much I value keeping a journal as you lean into significance, so let this book trigger your own thinking, and write down your thoughts. Then read what you have written. Read it to your spouse at night. Read it to yourself a month from now.

If you are reading this book, you have chosen to investigate a path that is far less traveled than the one you have been on. In reality, that path has chosen *you*, for something inside of you has already whispered that you can't keep doing what you're doing. These musings are my way of amplifying that still, small voice by walking with you along that path. I have never regretted stepping out into the unknown, and neither will you.

Welcome to the journey of your life.

CHAPTER 1

Life as a State
of Perpetual Disorder

Does it ever seem that life just won't fall into place the way you planned? I keep calendars, I make appointments, I have daily plans, weekly plans, plans for my whole life. I want to take charge of life — to be proactive. But much of the time, perhaps most of the time, my life and the lives of most of the people I know are much more spontaneous than our linear plans would describe.

Take this book, for instance. I have been trying to take my thoughts and musings about halftime and arrange them in an orderly, linear fashion, and it has been extremely frustrating. I'm not even sure it can be done. Management guru Peter Drucker once shocked me by saying, "People who plan are the unhappiest people in the world. Opportunity is unpredictable. Most of the time, opportunity comes in over the transom. And opportunity doesn't stay long. If you don't respond to an opportunity, it moves on." The same is true for problems. If you don't change plans and react, your problems just get worse. As Shakespeare said, "Readiness is all." Readiness and reaction are key.

So the nature of this book is spontaneous and reactive. Its content cannot really be put into a linear, step-by-step order. I tried it, and it didn't work, because my life — like yours I expect — just won't conform to my plans. It is messy, disorderly, one surprise after another.

My beautiful wife, Linda, has watched with bemused sympathy as I have twisted and turned in the breeze trying to solve this making-order-out-of-chaos issue. She came into my study at our farm one day to tell me that she was taking a course on the Psalms. She said, "Your musings don't have any order. They are more like psalms. They are reactions along the road of life. The Psalms are not theology. They are more how people relate to change." Then she read me the following poem from her friend Verdell Krisher:

Psalms

Are they poems Are they conflicting
Are they prayers Are they experiential
Are they praises Are they majestic
Are they songs Are they dark
Are they laments Are they intense
Are they personal Are they accusing
Are they communal Are they comforting
Yes.

The 150 psalms in the Bible are collected into five books with no seeming attempt given to order them by genre or history or author or anything else. Philip Yancey wrote, "The 150 psalms are as difficult, disordered, and messy as life itself."

If you are looking for chronological order in this book — or in your second-half journey — you will be disappointed with both. Life in the second half is disordered, surprising, and only occasionally as you plan it. And all of that contradiction is what makes it wonderful. I suspect when we are in our thirties, we just can't live with such disorderliness, which makes the transition feel so uncomfortable at times.

I have learned to embrace discomfort and to celebrate disorderliness. I have learned to trust the unknown that comes with abandoning the drive to succeed.

The psalmist understands our trepidation in leaving the known, the comfortable. When he entered a cave to flee King Saul he wrote:

> *Have mercy on me, my God, have mercy on me,*
> *for in you I take refuge.*
> *I will take refuge in the shadow of your wings*
> *until the disaster has passed.*
>
> *I cry out to God Most High,*
> *to God, who vindicates me.*
>
> *He sends from heaven and saves me,*
> *rebuking those who hotly pursue me —*
> *God sends forth his love and his faithfulness.*
>
> *I am in the midst of lions;*
> *I am forced to dwell among man-eating beasts,*
> *whose teeth are spears and arrows,*
> *whose tongues are sharp swords.*

Be exalted, O God, above the heavens;
let your glory be over all the earth.
Psalm 57:1–5 (TNIV)

My life was well-ordered pre-halftime. It had to be, for that is how we succeed. The inertia of orderliness still pulls heavily, but the unexpected interruptions soon become a refuge, allowing you to be who you were created to be. If you are feeling pressure right now to finish this chapter, write down your thoughts, set the book down, take a deep breath, and close your eyes. Then get back to the real work of your life.

This *is* the real world.

::

Reflection

Questions have always played a big role in my halftime journey, so I will be posing a few at the end of each chapter. My recommendation is that you read through them and select two or three that best fit your situation and write out your thoughts about them in a journal.

1. What movie, novel, song, poem, or quote would you pick to say, "That's just my situation now"? Or if you were to write a psalm expressing your current state of mind, what would it say?

2. Look over your calendar of the past two weeks. Describe an unpredicted event or conversation — something that was not according to plan. Were you upset when it happened? Were you still upset after it happened?

3. What have all the time-saving and time-management devices and techniques added to your life? What have they taken from your life? Which do you want more — what these devices have added to your life or what they have taken from your life?

4. Management expert Peter Drucker said that people who plan are the unhappiest people in the world. Think of someone you know who is a planner and someone else you know who is more spontaneous. Which person seems happiest to you? What qualities do you admire in each person?

5. If you were given a "free day" tomorrow, what would you do?

Wise Companions

"For I know the plans I have for you," declares the LORD, "plans to prosper you and not to harm you, plans to give you hope and a future."

JEREMIAH 29:11

"Do not worry about tomorrow, for tomorrow will worry about itself. Each day has enough trouble of its own."

MATTHEW 6:34

Humans have a thousand plans; Heaven has but one.

CHINESE PROVERB

CHAPTER 2

How to Know
When You're in Halftime

At least once a week, someone asks me, "How do I know I'm in halftime? How do I know when it's time to move on?" As the Kenny Rogers tune advises, "You gotta know when to hold 'em and know when to fold 'em." My response is always something like "You know when you know. Tell me your story."

The answer is always personal (it's the individual's answer, not mine); it's intuitive; and it's human. The answer comes from insight, not from analysis. You contemplate for a long while, and then all of a sudden you see "it." You see what the next move is! But it's been in your history a long, long time. Once you see a new future, the question shifts to "Will I do it?" or even more precisely, "Do I have the will to pull the trigger?"

One caution. Halftime is not a crisis. It is not a retreat from a high-stress job that is getting the best of you or an antidote for a difficult marriage. Halftime usually comes when you are at or near the top of your game but you just don't get the rush from success that you used to. You don't view your success negatively but have become indifferent to it.

A dramatic example of someone who stepped out of a hugely successful career to act on a more meaning-filled future is international chess champion Gary Kasparov. His story was recounted in the *Wall Street Journal*:

> Thirty years ago at the Soviet Junior Championship I played my first major chess event at the national level. Twenty years ago in Moscow I became the youngest World Champion in history. Last week in Spain I played my final serious games of chess, winning the Linares super-tournament for the ninth time. After three decades as a professional chess player, the last two ranked No. 1, I have decided to retire from professional chess.
>
> … I'm a man who needs a goal, and who wants to make a difference….
>
> I have always set ambitious goals, and I have been lucky enough to attain most of them. I have achieved everything there is to achieve in the chess arena. It had become unfulfilling repetition…. Meanwhile, there are other areas where I can still make a difference, where I can set new goals and find new channels for my energy. At the age of 41, I believe there is still much I can accomplish. My experiences in the chess world have provided me with an excellent foundation for these new challenges.
>
> … Ultimately it is my interest in politics that has played the principal role in my decision to reallocate

my resources away from chess. For many years, I have been an ardent supporter of democracy in Russia, and at certain times I have participated in political activities. Now I will be able to do this with the same determination and passion I brought to the chessboard.

I believe my talents and experience can be useful in the political realm. There is something to be said for a chess player's ability to see the whole board. Many politicians are so focused on one problem, or a single aspect of a problem, that they remain unaware that solving it may require action on something that appears unrelated. It is natural for a chess player, by contrast, to look at the big picture.

So now Kasparov is using his lifelong knowledge and passion to play chess on a larger board. He has had enough of success in one realm and seeks to find significance by entering politics. Talk about a big, hairy, audacious goal (B-HAG)! He didn't need anyone to tell him it was time to move on. He reached a point when what he had to do became quite clear — all that was left was the will to do it.

You probably already know what you need to do. Or at least that you have had your fill of success. If you listen, explore, pay attention to your passion, and dare to dream big, you will know what you have to do, and all that will be left is the will to do it.

Reflection

1. What has become "unfulfilling repetition" for you (even though you may have become very accomplished at it)?

2. What is your passion, something that causes you to lose all sense of time thinking about it, something you wish you could spend more time doing?

3. Where have your skills already been useful in a related field?

4. If money and time were not an issue, what's the biggest dream you have for doing something significant? Identify at least one small step you can take toward fulfilling that dream.

1) The "Sales" game
2) Mentoring young people about "living" a successful life.
3) Landmark, Marie, Ready for Life
4) Writing a book. like this one.
   Reading this book.

Wise Companions

God made us for joy. God is joy, and the joy of living reflects the original joy that God felt in creating us.

POPE JOHN PAUL II

You may be 38 years old, as I happen to be. And one day, some great opportunity stands before you and calls upon you to stand up for some great principle, some great issue, some great cause. And you refuse to do it because you are afraid. You refuse to do it because you want to live longer. You're afraid that you will lose your job, or you're afraid that you will be criticized or that you will lose your popularity, or you're afraid that somebody will stab you, or shoot at you or bomb your house; so you refuse to take the stand. Well you may go on and live until you are 90, but you're just as dead at 38 as you would be at 90. And the cessation of breathing in your life is but the belated announcement of an earlier death of the spirit. You died when you refused to stand up for right. You died when you refused to stand up for truth. You refused to stand up for justice.

DR. MARTIN LUTHER KING JR.,
from the sermon "But, If Not" delivered
at Ebenezer Baptist Church, Atlanta,
November 5, 1967, five months
before his assassination

CHAPTER 3

Defining Moments

In *Halftime* I stress the importance of lifelong learning. It's one of the six goals I set for myself at age thirty-four. It is said that school is wasted on the young. In our youth we just don't have enough experience for knowledge to lead to understanding. For me, critical insights into life come through the intersection of literature (plays, poems, books) and current events in different seasons of my life. My friend Dr. Larry Allums, a humanities professor, leads me through great literature by assigning me a book or play every two weeks. I make copious notes, comparing my personal situations with the dramatic situations faced by the characters in the reading. It's like psychoanalysis through great literature. I look at a recent personal experience in the light of someone else's responses to life's challenges, and that falls in the category of lifelong learning.

Linda and I had been in England for two weeks. I used a board meeting in London as an excuse for us to drive twelve hundred miles amid radiantly green pastures separated by miles of rock walls in the Cotswolds and the Lake Country. It was a gorgeous time of year — cool mornings among green pastures filled with lots of sheep. We had never been so far north in Britain and reveled in discovering many small, stone-clad villages, mysterious stone circles, and warm, cozy pubs for shepherd's pie and plowman's lunch.

The absolute highlight of the trip for me was to experience (it's the only way to say it) Ian McKellen playing the lead role in the Royal Shakespeare Company stage production of *King Lear*. We had been trying unsuccessfully to get tickets for months and just by pure luck happened into two perfect seats (five rows from the stage) in the split-second availability after a cancellation the night before the play. Amazing and pure good fortune.

The central issue in *King Lear* is how an aging monarch, having lived in luxury, transitions to the next stage of his life. In the first act, Lear declares his intention:

> *'Tis our fast intent*
> *To shake all cares and business from our age;*
> *Conferring them on younger strengths,*
> *While we unburden'd crawl toward death.*

In other words, Lear seeks to retire from responsibility. The short summary of the next three and a half hours of agonizingly tragic drama is that Lear makes a total mess of this transition — ceding his property to his two daughters, Regan and Goneril — who are perhaps the two meanest creatures ever to inhabit stage or film — and disinheriting his loyal daughter, Cordelia, who refuses to make a flattering declaration of love like her two sisters. As they say, "all hell breaks loose" as Lear, now stripped of his power, is thrown out by the two malicious daughters into a fiercely stormy night on the heath.

This was the second time *Lear*, perhaps Shakespeare's greatest play, has provided me with a defining moment in a time of decision. The first time was twenty or so years ago during my fortysomething halftime season. I was considering whether to retire from the television business I had led for a dozen years in order to devote full-time to Leadership Network (www.leadnet.org), which was drawing me away from the "success" season of my life toward what I felt was more meaningful work. During that decision time, I attended a panel discussion of *King Lear* at the University of Dallas, led by Dr. Louise Cowan and featuring a younger Dr. Larry Allums, then Louise's star protégé. Seeing how Lear had made a complete botch of leadership transition, I decided, "No way!" That play had a lot to do with my staying in business for the next twenty years. Instead of retiring, I, with my brothers' blessing, reorganized the management of Buford Television so that I became chairman of the board. Leadership of the operating company was taken over by a competent, energetic, and pretested management team. I continued as an owner with a voice in a few key strategic and personnel decisions. Yet, unlike Lear, I didn't give up the keys to the kingdom. I became what is now called a nonexecutive chairman of the board. Lear taught me that lesson.

So what lesson did I learn watching *Lear* in the Lake Country of England? What changed for this later season of my life? What decision was on the table as I was held in rapt attention by the 2007 Stratford-upon-Avon version of Shakespeare's great play? The experience reaffirmed for me and strengthened my resolve that retirement just doesn't work for me. Maybe it doesn't work for anybody. We are wired for purposeful human engagement and contribution, and without it, we wither. In this fresh season of my life, I'm reorganizing not retiring. My new determination is "purposeful life until the last breath." That's what is on my T-shirt now. Call it life coaching by Shakespeare!

Most of us are required to read *King Lear* sometime in our formal schooling, but we miss the point. We are too young and do not have enough life experience to recognize that most great stories are versions of the universal human story. That's why a "continuing education" program — formal or informal — is so important in halftime.

By the way, the biblical version of this Shakespearean tragedy is King Solomon in the Old Testament book of Ecclesiastes. I read that book every year. That's another story for another day, but the moral of the story is the same: life without purpose is not living at all.

Reflection

1. Think of a recent novel or movie that had an impact on you. In what ways did you relate to the main character or a supporting character? How did the story change your perspective?

2. Aside from work-related learning and study, what are you doing to engage your mind and continue learning for the sake of personal edification? What percentage of your reading includes fiction, drama, or poetry?

3. Who is the most influential wisdom figure in your life — a coach, mentor, or friend with whom you can "think your confusion out loud"? List two or three ways this person has influenced you.

4. King Lear made a mess of dividing his kingdom among his children. What will you do differently when it comes to making similar decisions for your family?

Wise Companions

By three methods we may learn wisdom: First, by reflection, which is noblest; second, by imitation, which is easiest; and third, by experience, which is the bitterest.

CONFUCIUS

Q: This is your third go at *Lear*. You've done two major productions of it, first in 1968 and then in 1976. You've had now thirty-some odd years to think about it. How much has your thinking about the play changed?

A: Thirty-some odd years in the *second half* rather than the first half of my life. So Shakespeare engaging with questions about mortality and what we construct for ourselves either to explain or to accept our mortality, speaks very potently to me now. [emphasis mine]

From an interview with TREVOR NUNN,
who directed King Lear at Stratford

When I applied my mind to know wisdom and to observe the labor that is done on earth — people getting no sleep day or night — then I saw all that God has done.

ECCLESIASTES 8:16–17

CHAPTER 4

The Metrics
of Significance

How do you measure significance? I spent a morning recently preparing to speak to a Young Presidents' Organization (YPO) chapter in Chicago. I knew this audience well, having been a member of YPO and having spoken at several of their functions. This particular group was obviously taking my talk seriously: They had hired a college professor to cross-examine me in Q&A fashion, sent copies of *Halftime* to all the participants, and even prepared a three-page outline of questions. The final question from this audience of "rich young rulers" went something like this: "In American society, we generally agree on the measures of success (financial independence/security, material possessions, etc.). However, when it comes to significance, we don't have an agreed-upon set of metrics to refer to. How, then, does one measure significance?"

This is a serious question, and a fair one, since I have been asking people to make the switch from success to significance. I believe a lot of people stick with business and secular work because there is a clear scorekeeping mechanism. You win or lose. You make the deal or someone else does. You get rich or go broke. Clear metrics.

I define success as "using your knowledge and experience to build up your own portfolio (metrics)." The technique for significance is similar. It's the mission that is different. I define it as "using your knowledge and experience to serve others"; and by serving others, you serve God. Peter Drucker defines the "end results" of a nonprofit or ministry as "changed lives": "Its product is a changed human being. The nonprofit institutions are human change agents. Their 'product' is a cured patient, a child that learns, a young man or woman grown into a self-respecting adult; a changed human life altogether."[1]

Success is mostly about externals. In *The American Idea of Success*, Richard Huber defines success as three things: money, fame, and power. Matthew's gospel describes how Jesus was tempted after forty days in the wilderness (Matthew 4:1–11). I have always thought that the three temptations in this profound and universal story (satisfy your hunger, do something spectacular, and take power over the kingdoms of the world) were pretty similar to those that emerged out of Huber's extensive research — the same temptations two thousand years apart. Nothing changes.

Significance is defined more personally and internally. It is an existential choice. It is about what we want to do with our lives when success gives us freedom of action and choice, and for most people living in the developed world, there is enough freedom to do both.

But the choice to serve others is entirely ours. The theological term is "free will." It's up to us. There is no economic incentive. The outcomes are much more diverse. There is no "generally agreed upon" measure as the YPO questioner put it, other than "changed lives." Can they be measured? I think they can. But doing so is personal and subjective. It's like the man who tried to describe hope: "I can't explain it, but I know it when I have it." Or as Peter Drucker told me once, "You can't always measure it, but you can know it."

Reflection

1. A common sentiment of people in halftime is "I spent my entire first half keeping score. In my second half, I don't want to keep score. I just want to do something that gives my life more meaning." Why do you think "keeping score" becomes less important as we get older?

2. What are your personal standards of success? In other words, how do you keep score in your work life? How do you measure up to those standards?

3. Is measuring significance as important to you as measuring success? If it's not, do you wish it were?

4. Do you have a way to measure significance in your life? If not, what measures might you choose? How will you know if you have achieved significance?

5. What is your second-half mission, and how will that give you significance?

1) The first half is proving you can do it. The second is what to do with that proof - what value is it unless you share it - pass it on.

2. Happiness, self fulfillment awareness that I make a difference.

3. yes it is as significant.

4. when I feel moved by acknowledgment.

5. I want to change lives - create new possibility

Wise Companions

He who cannot draw on three thousand years is living from hand to mouth.

GOETHE

Two roads diverged in a yellow wood,
And sorry I could not travel both
And be one traveler, long I stood
And looked down one as far as I could
To where it bent in the undergrowth;

Then took the other, as just as fair,
And having perhaps the better claim,
Because it was grassy and wanted wear;
Though as for that the passing there
Had worn them really about the same,

And both that morning equally lay
In leaves no step had trodden black.
Oh, I kept the first for another day!
Yet knowing how way leads on to way,
I doubted if I should ever come back.

I shall be telling this with a sigh
Somewhere ages and ages hence:
Two roads diverged in a wood, and I —
I took the one less traveled by,
And that has made all the difference.

ROBERT FROST, "The Road Not Taken"

CHAPTER 5

Too Much
of a Good Thing?

I have always said, "Better is always better." But lately I have been asking myself, *Is this really true?* Ambition is a good thing. Hard work is a good thing. Leisure, rest, and play are good things. But there are limits to each. Let me tell you what has drawn me up short, got me thinking a lot about boundaries and limits. Following is a story of two good men, men whose work I know and respect — virtuous men whose lives have been spent serving God's purposes and serving others. We have a ceaseless barrage of television news about bad guys who lie, cheat, steal, and break the rules in a variety of nasty ways. But I'm talking about good guys. Most of the people I know mean well. They lead purposeful lives and intend to do so until the last breath, just as these two men did.

But both found themselves beyond their limits.

Both men are senior pastors. Both are very gifted communicators and are loved and respected by the people they serve. Actually, they are held in awe. Both of them are in their fifties, leading churches with more than two thousand attending each week. Think of the pressure of that job. First of all, they have the pressure of preparing and delivering a message to thousands of people each week and of being very much in the spotlight. That, combined with the leadership responsibility of what is essentially a very large service enterprise, is hugely demanding.

The first pastor leads a church in the western United States. He began the church himself and is well-known as a writer and a person who does leadership seminars for many other pastors. Not long ago, I heard him give a message to pastors describing his experience of burnout. He said he had gotten to a point where he felt like he was faking everything. He described it this way:

> I felt "fried inside." I lost enthusiasm for what I was doing. The work that had been a great passion for me had become just a job. I was dragging myself through each day. I knew something was wrong, talked to a couple of friends about it, and finally sought medical help. The doctor diagnosed burnout and prescribed six months of rest — absolutely no work. It was that bad.
>
> I said "no way," but I did book right away a short silent retreat in a Catholic monastery. It wasn't perfect, but it gave me enough relief to at least think deeply about what was happening to me and to take steps to make myself accountable to my family and to those I worked with for a much easier work schedule. I delegated responsibility for all manner of things to subordinates who did a terrific job.

The second pastor leads a large church on the opposite side of the country, and he, too, began to experience burnout. A number of people in his congregation had predicted it. He was very detail oriented and reluctant to delegate anything. He was operating a large church as if it were a small parish church, doing lots of pastoral care and preparing messages each week. He was a micromanager. He began to feel some physical pain, and, as a result, took painkillers that soon led to a deep addiction to prescription drugs. As it was discovered later, he had multiple doctors in his congregation prescribing for him strong and addictive prescription drugs, not knowing others were doing the same. He was like a duck that appears calm on the surface and paddles like crazy under the water just to stay afloat.

The people on his board felt clearly that something was wrong and thought that they should hire more help for him. One of them later said, "We were treating the wrong disease in the wrong way, but how were we to know?" Things finally came to a head when the truth about his addiction found its way onto the front page of the local newspaper. People were shocked. The minister was temporarily relieved of his senior pastor duties and entered a six-month regimen in a treatment center and halfway house.

The pastor in the first case is fully recovered and has restored his spiritual vitality and his passion and energy for work. He has been willing to talk about his issue with groups of pastors in the hope that he will "warn them in time." The pastor in the second case has found work in another field. There's hope. He is a very intelligent man who has taken steps to restore his relationship with his family and with others whom he served. But he's not out of the woods yet.

I asked Dr. Larry Allums, my "personal trainer in literature," about this issue. He told me that a great deal of literature and drama turns around "the tragic flaw" — characters not admitting their limits to themselves or others. In Shakespeare, Julius Caesar is a great general and a very poor politician. King Lear is so blinded by his own self-absorption and desire to retire and take it easy that he is careless about putting his kingdom and his own future in good hands.

The tragic flaw in the case of the two pastors was their unwillingness to admit their limits and to acknowledge their need for others as the demands of their work scaled up so dramatically.

Halftime is not about burnout, but some people who enter this transition period continue to ignore their tragic flaws. Sadly, they are the ones who never make it to the second half. One of the most important things for you to do in halftime is to honestly examine yourself. Face those things about you that need to change, and then set about changing them.

Reflection

1. What secrets, big or small, do you keep from your spouse or closest friend? What keeps you from sharing those things?

2. Do you agree that everyone has a "tragic flaw"? If so, what is yours? What would your closest friend or spouse say your tragic flaw is?

3. Have you experienced burnout? What was it like for you? How did you deal with it? What changes did you make?

4. Some people find it necessary to be one person at work, another person at home, and yet another person in private. To what degree is this true for you? In which of the three areas are you most authentically yourself?

5. The *Aspen Times* has on its front page each day "If you don't want to see it in print, don't let it happen." Good advice. What would you not like to see in print?

Wise Companions

Hypocrisy and distortion are passing currents under the name of religion.

MAHATMA GANDHI

We are only falsehood, duplicity, contradiction; we both conceal and disguise ourselves from ourselves.

BLAISE PASCAL

Self-deception helps us deceive.

DAVID LIVINGSTONE

Whoever walks in integrity walks securely, but whoever takes crooked paths will be found out.

PROVERBS 10:9

CHAPTER 6

Discarding the Past, Moving On!

Have you ever moved? Whether moving into a new home or into a new office, moving is a lot of work. But it's also a great opportunity to unload all the stuff you've accumulated but don't really need. Several months ago Leadership Network moved its offices. The move was only about three blocks east, overlooking the Quadrangle in Dallas, but the short distance didn't make it much easier. My capable assistant, BJ Engle, and I are incorrigible pack rats. We save everything! So I spent a full day poking into drawers, corners, and file folders filled with ten years' worth of stuff. I sorted through and threw away many of the paper artifacts of my past, and I learned a few things in the process.

The past is the past. It will never come again. They say you never put your foot in the same river twice, because the water has moved downstream. I threw away seven kitchen-sized plastic wastebaskets of paper that represented ten years of work. The next morning it was in a landfill. And it seemed so important to me at one time.

Why did I save all this stuff? I have a friend who went into a near panic because he accidentally and permanently deleted more than two hundred emails he had not yet answered. But within a few days he realized his business hadn't collapsed — in fact, no one seemed to notice his lack of response. Maybe what we save is not all that important after all.

The past clogs up the future. Living in the past is like walking in quicksand. It inhibits your mobility, your freedom of action to respond to today. It's about what was, not what is. That day of throwing away "important papers" made me recall that, in business, I often started an acquisition drive by divesting a property we had fully developed. That's a pretty good rule for filing things away — for every piece of paper you file, throw another piece away.

Hitting foul balls and drilling dry holes are part of life. I threw away a ton of back issues of *Halftime* magazine, the residue of its three-issue life. It was an exciting run that, in essence, taught me the difference between being an editor and being a writer, knowledge I put to work doing my fourth book, *Finishing Well.* At the time, the magazine seemed like a great idea, and maybe it was. But it died a slow death. I threw away other reminders of false starts. It's good to be reminded that much of what we do has a beginning and an end, and that's okay. Never let your failures live beyond their death.

You have to swing at lots of pitches to hit home runs. One Leadership Network program, for which I partnered with Phil Anschutz and some others, convened a group of

American megachurches that planted 1,650 new churches and held 1,100 teaching events for thousands of other church leaders over the past six years. Just in the United States! It's remarkable what happens when you convert latent energy to active energy. But if I had given up every time I started something that didn't work out as I had planned, our megachurch program may never have gotten off the ground.

When I began a parallel career in 1984 by establishing Leadership Network, our objective was to help fast-growing churches grow even faster. Back then there were very few churches with more than one thousand attending — our initial definition of a megachurch. According to a report released February 3, 2006, by Dave Travis of Leadership Network and Scott Thumma of Hartford Institute for Religion Research, there are now 1,210 megachurches, each with two thousand or more weekly attendees. These churches draw nearly 4.4 million people a week and collect $7 billion a year in donations. That accomplishment might not have sunk in had I not taken a day to clear out my files. Intentional reflection is a good thing.

You are not in control of the universe. Life is a multifactor equation. It has lots of moving parts, and I'm just one of them. I found that most of what I had in mind worked out after awhile. But much of it certainly wasn't according to the original plan in terms of how I went about it. As they say, "Man proposes. God disposes."

Significance is a calling to be a part of a cause greater than yourself. This calling has been the central focus of my life for the past twenty years. For that I have no regrets. None. In a conversation several years ago with Peter Drucker, I heard myself lamenting "how much money I had left on the table" by focusing on the work I felt God had called me to do instead of growing my business. He said, "Yes, but you had your life these past fifteen years." He made me see that meaning trumped money, and that creating the margin and balance in my life to move on to my "grown-up" occupation was what made space for what was important rather than what was urgent.

Mentors are of great value. Clearing out old files reminded me of how important mentors are. Few realize the impact of Peter Drucker's thinking on the church. I have acres of notes and tapes of our conversations, many that included intimate dialogue between Peter and some of the most recognized pastors in America. He never really liked being known as the "father of modern management," insisting that his real contribution was about people and their potential. I'm glad I kept all of the Peter files. He is gone physically, but what a legacy of wisdom, advice, and example he has left me — enough to guide me for the next twenty years, and that ought to be plenty.

The physical act of moving my office helped me see that some things in my past need to be discarded; some things need to be kept and treasured. One day of slowing down and handling both types of artifacts forced me to reflect on the various seasons of my life. Maybe we shouldn't wait for a move to do that.

Reflection

1. Try to identify two or three things from your past that seemed like a good idea at the time but ended up less than successful. What did you learn from them? What is your attitude toward those things? Do they trouble or embarrass you, or are you able to leave them behind?

2. Looking back on your life, divide your time into three or four seasons. Then think of a word or phrase that best describes each. What might the label for your next season be? Explain your logic in labeling these seasons to a spouse, a good friend, or your small group. Do they agree? Try to look at your life reflected in their mirrors.

3. Identify three or four things from your past that deserve to be treasured. Spend some time reflecting on them, even on the details. What makes these things so valuable to you?

4. On your next business trip, take a file of some of your oldest correspondence. As you read each letter, compare your life now with what it was when you received that letter. How has it changed? How would you respond now to some of those letters?

Wise Companions

*For everything its season, and for every activity under
   heaven its time:*
a time to be born and a time to die;
a time to plant and a time to uproot;
a time to kill and a time to heal;
a time to pull down and a time to build up;
a time to weep and a time to laugh;
a time for mourning and a time for dancing;
a time to scatter stones and a time to gather them;
a time to embrace and a time to refrain from embracing;
a time to seek and a time to lose;
a time to keep and a time to throw away;
a time to tear and a time to mend;
a time for silence and a time for speech;
a time to love and a time to hate;
a time for war and a time for peace.
What profit does one who works get from all his labour?
   *I have seen the business that God has given men to
   keep them busy. He has made everything to suit its
   time; moreover he has given men a sense of time past
   and future, but no comprehension of God's work from
   beginning to end.*

                                   Ecclesiastes 3:1 – 11 NEB

CHAPTER 7

Dancing with the Gorilla

A man called me the other day to ask my advice. As I always do, I said, "Tell me your story." This man, let's call him Alex, went on to say that twenty or so years ago he had been one of hundreds of ambitious young partners to work for my friend Don Williams in the glory days of the Trammell Crow Company, which grew quickly to become the largest commercial developer in the 1980s' real estate boom. It was a run-fast, get-rich time until the government abruptly changed the rules late in the game, creating chaos in the markets. Nine of the ten largest Texas banks failed as lease rates and real estate asset values collapsed like a pin pricking an overinflated balloon. I was in a small group with Don in Dallas in those heady days. It was a nerve-racking season. Partnerships that had been easy to form became agonizingly difficult to unwind. Don was the steady hand at the tiller of a ship threatening to break up in a storm.

As Trammell Crow transitioned from a network of loosely connected partnerships focused on building capital values to a public company managing assets for a fee, Alex and many other young partners found themselves out on the street. Alex told me, "It was awful at the time but probably the best thing that ever happened to me." He and a group of others began a new real estate development venture that grew from scratch to a current market capitalization of $30 billion. Alex progressed to CEO of the company, a position he now holds.

I had given counsel several years ago to another boom-and-bust entrepreneur as he had watched $100 million evaporate in a market crash. He lived in the same town with Alex. After hearing Alex's story, the entrepreneur gave him two recommendations: get out while you're ahead, and call Bob Buford about what to do with the rest of your life. Alex, now more than well-off, said he had grown weary of the intensity and relentless pace of doing real estate deals, but (1) he didn't quite know how to get off the merry-go-round, and (2) though he felt an inner calling to do something about his well-nourished Christian faith, he didn't have the least idea of where to start. Those were his issues.

I recalled an old saying, one that had been like an audio loop in my mind when I, too, in my halftime season, decided I wanted to make the change from success to significance as the primary loyalty in my life. The refrain was like this: "If you're dancing with a gorilla, you can't stop dancing 'til the gorilla decides to stop."

I wanted to stop dancing then. Alex wanted to stop now. But how? How do you know when you have enough? In my case, I had the lead role in a prosperous, growing television company. As I said in my musings about *King*

Lear, I was able to transition the leadership of Buford Television to recapture and reallocate 80 percent of my time to my Christian calling. I came to call this a parallel career. It took me eight years to get me where I wanted to be.

Linda and I answered the "How much is enough?" question after our only heir and son, Ross, died in a tragic accident in 1987. In what I came to call "a reverse tithe," we set aside an amount for the two of us to live (quite comfortably) on. Then, with Linda's support, I committed myself to disburse the rest in the noble causes that now engage my skills and passion during my lifetime. If Ross had lived, I would have set aside an amount to get him started in life and done the same. We were already embarked when events altered our timetable.

In the case of Alex, he has told his board that he wants to make an orderly transition out of the CEO role. They have asked for two more years, which seems reasonable to me and to him. Like so many others, actually most of the halftimers I talk to, Alex doesn't have any idea of what significance cause he will be drawn to. But also like most others, he will begin to make a few low-cost probes to begin to see what reignites his passion in this new season of life. If Alex is available and openhanded with his life, God will illumine a path as he has done for others.

How do you know when you have enough? When you get tired of dancing with the gorilla. Our human nature drives us to want more, leading us to put off significance until we have enough money, success, or achievement.

Reflection

1. Beginning sometime in their forties, most people experience some degree of weariness in their accomplishments and begin to desire "something else." Yet they generally keep "dancing with the gorilla." Why do you think it is so hard to leave success for something better?

2. Try to quantify these three areas of your life in terms of how important they are to you: money, success, achievement. What are the good things that have come from those areas? What are the costs?

3. How would your life be better if you had more money, success, and achievement than you now have? Are you enjoying the "dance" required to obtain more in these areas?

4. If your life worked out perfectly, what would be the "priceless" elements of that life? What are the things that cannot be replaced with money, success, or achievement?

5. Share your answers to these questions with your spouse or closest friend, and invite that person to answer the same questions. Were you surprised at the similarity or dissimilarity of that person's answers?

Wise Companions

"Do not store up for yourselves treasures on earth, where moth and rust destroy, and where thieves break in and steal. But store up for yourselves treasures in heaven, where moth and rust do not destroy, and where thieves do not break in and steal. For where your treasure is, there your heart will be also....
"No one can serve two masters. Either you will hate the one and love the other, or you will be devoted to the one and despise the other. You cannot serve both God and Money."

Matthew 6:19–21, 24

I also have in my mind that seemingly wealthy, but most terribly impoverished class of all, who have accumulated dross, but know not how to use it, or get rid of it, and thus have forged their own golden or silver fetters.

Henry David Thoreau, Walden

Money often costs too much.

Ralph Waldo Emerson

CHAPTER 8

The Gift of Silence

I find that the longer I live, the more I value silence. Pure, unadulterated silence. Absence of noise. White space. Blank canvas.

Two years ago, as a gift to recognize my sixty-five years of active life and as an investment in my extended halftime, I gave myself one extra free day each week. I don't intend to retire. Ever! Work is a psychological necessity to me. If I'm not contributing, I begin to feel pretty worthless — fast. A lack of contributing is like an accusing shadow. I like being with people, particularly capable people, a great deal. But I also have a monkish side that values silence, so I decided to program silence into my weekly schedule.

In lieu of working completely, then retiring completely, my rhythm now is to do the work I feel called to do Monday through Thursday. Friday through Sunday are free days — days when I go to a place that gives me permission to be free and unstructured, usually Still Point Farm in East Texas. But sometimes Linda and I find a beautiful hideaway in another part of the country and spend our free days there.

For example, awhile ago, in conjunction with a working trip to New York, we consulted *The Hideaway Report* to discover Castle on the Hudson in a small town in upstate New York. We spent an afternoon walking the trails of the thousand-acre Rockefeller estate. The air was crisp. The trees had turned remarkable blazing reds and yellows, rich oranges and browns. It was a weekday, and we were virtually by ourselves. The park ranger said it was the best day of the season. We spoke very little, just crunched along those forest trails hand in hand.

Two days later I was at lunch in New York City's ultimate power restaurant, the Four Seasons, with two Wall Street friends trying to conceive what we might do together to serve our better sides. It is an electrifying place: soaring Mies van der Rohe architecture, tables commanded by titans — Jack Welch over there, Joe Montana across the room, Sanford Weill wheeling and dealing close by. New York City!

But it seems I'm always happiest to get back to Still Point Farm. The great gift here is silence. Freedom from compulsion and necessity. The ability to let go, to let things happen instead of making things happen.

Here I see more clearly. Here things come together. Here experience, knowledge, memory, the Holy Spirit, and great books merge in wondrous and surprising ways. Poetry makes sense. The content of silence is much more in the realm of faith and intuition than in the realm of reason. Almost mysteriously, silence helps us make sense of the seemingly disparate thoughts and events in our lives.

Thomas Merton says to me in my devotional time things like this: "It is not thoughts that matter, but hours of silence and the precious dimension of existence which is otherwise completely unknown.... If only [we] could realize that nothing has to be uttered. The silence that is printed in the center of our being. It will not fail us. It is more than silence. Jesus spoke of the spring of living water, you remember."[2]

My journal says in response, "Yes, that's it. It is more than silence. Much more. It is the precious gift of seeing. Seeing what is. Not ever being silent; not seeing, except through the eyes of his own predisposition, was King Lear's tragic flaw."

Watching a PBS program from the American Masters series about Albert Einstein, I heard the great physicist quoted as saying: "Look, look deep into nature and then you will understand everything. As I grow older, the identification with the here and now is slowly lost. One feels dissolved and merged into nature. It makes me feel happy. The greatest experience we can have is the mysterious."

Later on in the same program, former Israeli ambassador Abba Eban described a conversation with Einstein: "He said the religious idea must not be dismissed, because he himself has found that there is a realm beyond which human understanding stands impotent and helpless."

In the silence, I heard this echo from scripture and memory: "Faith is the substance of things hoped for, the evidence of things not seen" (Heb. 11:1 KJV).

And then Linda and I were watching an interview with

Barack Obama about his book *The Audacity of Hope*. We heard him saying in the commonsense way he has of speaking, "Faith is, by definition, about things that can't be proved. Government is about things that are concrete, things that must be subject to proof."[3]

And the next morning, I was back to Thomas Merton again, who echoed a version of the same idea as Einstein, Obama, and the apostle Paul. "Actually, one decides one's life by responding to a word that is not well defined, easily explicable, safely accounted for. One decides to love in the face of an unaccountable void, and from the void comes an unaccountable truth. By this truth one's existence is sustained in peace." In other words, when we relinquish our need for certainty, we are more likely to discover the truth about our lives.

When we take time to be silent, thoughts converge. The dots begin to connect. There is resonance between the quiet voice of a hermit monk, the world's most famous physicist, an emerging political superstar, and the apostle Paul of two thousand years ago. That's what comes, not from the make-things-happen world of Monday through Thursday, but in the silence of a crisp, cold morning at Still Point Farm. Where does this happen for you?

Annie Dillard captures the idea of waiting patiently for an idea to be made clear in the following magical passage from *Pilgrim at Tinker Creek*:

> The secret of seeing is, then, the pearl of great price. If I thought he could teach me to find it and keep it

forever I would stagger barefoot across a hundred deserts after any lunatic at all. But although the pearl may be found it may not be sought. The literature of illumination reveals this above all: although it comes to those who wait for it, it is always, even to the most practiced and adept, a gift and a total surprise.... I cannot cause light; the most I can do is try to put myself in the path of its beam. It is possible, in deep space, to sail on solar wind. Light, be it particle or wave, has force: you rig a giant sail and go. The secret of seeing is to sail on solar wind. Hone and spread your spirit till you yourself are a sail, whetted, translucent, broadside to the merest puff.

You may not be in a position to give yourself one full day of silence each week. Yet. So start with an hour, a morning, an afternoon. It was in a brief, silent moment that you heard the still, small voice. Give it more space and time, and it will keep speaking to you.

Reflection

1. Does the need for silence I have described make sense or sound like it is from another universe? (In a way, it is.) Why?

2. Many people avoid periods of silence because they are afraid of what they might think or feel if they sit still long enough. Others claim they are too busy to get any "quiet time." What tends to keep you from having enough silence in your life?

3. During the last week or month, have you deliberately spent any time alone, in silence, with no agenda other than to listen, think, and observe? If you did, how did it affect you? Was it enriching? Awkward? A waste of time?

4. Where are the one or two places on earth that give you permission to be in silence? What voices emerge for you in the silence?

5. What prevents you from having regular, intentional times of silence? What would it take to program more silence into your life?

Wise Companions

Then a great and powerful wind tore the mountains apart and shattered the rocks before the Lord, but the Lord was not in the wind. After the wind there was an earthquake, but the Lord was not in the earthquake. After the earthquake came a fire, but the Lord was not in the fire. And after the fire came a gentle whisper.

1 Kings 19:11–12

My soul, wait silently for God alone,
For my expectation is from Him.
… my refuge, is in God.

Psalm 62:5–7 NKJV

Every now and then go away, even briefly, for when you come back to your work your judgment will be surer; since to remain constantly at work will cause you to lose power.

Attributed to Leonardo da Vinci

CHAPTER 9

A Balanced Life

S ometimes small things, unexpected things, surprising things can make a difference in our lives. Mostly they seem to pass unnoticed as we pursue our 100X big deals. I find this distressingly the case for me most of the time. Linda says I'm too concerned with numbers. Maybe it's a guy thing to keep our emotions in check and not let the small things through. In the rush of completing endless to-do lists, we don't even "see" the small things.

Recently two "small things" happened to me that I let get through my stoic screening mechanism. One was an email that unexpectedly overwhelmed me. I allowed some private tears. The other was a visit.

The email was forwarded by Ron Fournier, the chief political reporter for the Associated Press in Washington, D.C. I have been networking him to some interesting sources for a book he has been working on about the intersection of new things in business, politics, and religion. Here's the email he forwarded:

> Recently, I overheard a mother and daughter in their last moments together at the airport. They had

announced the departure. Standing near the security gate, they hugged, and the mother said, "I love you and I wish you enough." The daughter replied, "Mom, our life together has been more than enough. Your love is all I ever needed. I wish you enough, too, Mom."

They kissed and the daughter left. The mother walked over to the window where I was seated. Standing there, I could see she wanted and needed to cry. I tried not to intrude on her privacy, but she welcomed me in by asking, "Did you ever say good-bye to someone knowing it would be forever?"

"Yes, I have," I replied. "Forgive me for asking, but why is this a forever good-bye?"

She answered, "I am old, and she lives so far away. I have challenges ahead, and the reality is, the next trip back will be for my funeral."

"When you were saying good-bye, I heard you say, 'I wish you enough.' May I ask what that means?"

She began to smile. "That's a wish that has been handed down from other generations. My parents used to say it to everyone." She paused a moment and looked up, as if trying to remember it in detail, and she smiled even more. "When we said, 'I wish you enough,' we were wanting the other person to have a life filled with just enough good things to sustain them." Then, turning toward me, she shared the following as if she were reciting it from memory.

I wish you enough sun to keep your attitude bright.
I wish you enough rain to appreciate the sun more.

I wish you enough happiness to keep your spirit alive.
I wish you enough pain so that the smallest joys in life
   appear much bigger.
I wish you enough gain to satisfy your wanting.
I wish you enough loss to appreciate all that you possess.
I wish you enough hellos to get you through the final
   good-bye.

She then began to cry and walked away.

They say it takes a minute to find a special person, an hour to appreciate them, a day to love them, but then an entire life to forget them.

Receiving an email like that strengthens my resolve never to hit the delete button until I have read the entire message. I was struck by the wisdom that surrounds us and thankful that Ron engaged this woman rather than give her the business traveler's polite cold shoulder.

The second event was a visit from David Bussau. A remarkable social entrepreneur, David was a pioneer in the microlending field, founding Opportunities International, a network of forty-one partners in twenty-seven countries providing opportunities for people in poverty to transform their lives. He is currently engaged in enterprise development in the tsunami-hit area of Indonesia and, of all places, in North Korea. He is a practical saint.

An extraordinarily quiet and low-key man, David was on my calendar at 9:00 a.m. for what I assumed was a "just passing through" visit combined with lots of other things in Dallas. We have been working on Leadership Network

Australia for churches in his country, a definitely tough sell in a country where only 5 percent set foot inside a church even once a year. We touched on that, but there was no real agenda or business on his mind, and we pretty much just talked like two old friends. After a couple of hours, David took me by surprise when he said, "Well, I've taken enough of your time. I came to the United States to receive an award yesterday in Los Angeles as a social entrepreneur, but I came here last night just to see you. I'm going back to Australia this afternoon." I was astonished, just astonished. Apparently the visit was just relational, a "small thing." I didn't have cancer or any other urgent reason for him to make a special trip, and he didn't ask for more money at the end. He just shook hands and disappeared down the elevator. I was at a loss for words.

The next morning, I emailed the following to David:

I'm still processing your visit yesterday. That you would come all the way from Los Angeles to spend a couple of hours with me is unusual to say the least. I am much honored by that. Perhaps it is as important to be privately honored as publicly honored. The scale of what you have done and continue to do — Opportunities International, Indonesia, North Korea — is so different than spending two days of your life to just come and talk. I, who traffic a good deal in words these days, am having difficulty describing what that visit meant. Let's just say I am honored, encouraged, and grateful for your friendship.

I doubt I will soon forget David's visit. It's the kind of thing that wakes you up at 2:00 a.m. asking, "Now what was that all about?" And yet, if we believe that people are more important than plans and that relationships matter, why should these "small things" surprise us? What would happen if we spent more time giving and receiving small things?

Reflection

1. When colleagues poke their head in your office just to say hello, how do you typically respond? Are you more likely to consider it an interruption or a small blessing? Do you have a tendency to move them along with a polite greeting, or do you invite them in and spend a few minutes chatting?

2. Make a short list of the special people in your life. What makes them so special to you? What "small things" might you do to express your gratitude for their roles in your life?

3. Some people have difficulty dropping their emotional guards when they receive expressions of kindness or generosity. Is that your typical response? If so, what is it you are guarding yourself against?

4. Make a list of all the "small things" you have received from others over the past several weeks. Are you surprised at the length or brevity of the list? What effect did each of those small things have on you?

5. What are your "stoic screening mechanisms" that are switched on when someone does something nice for you? What might happen if you switched them off?

Wise Companions

"Where two or three are gathered together in My name, I am there in the midst of them."

MATTHEW 18:20 NKJV

"She poured perfume on my body beforehand to prepare for my burial. Truly I tell you, wherever the gospel is preached throughout the world, what she has done will also be told, in memory of her."

MARK 14:8–9

CHAPTER 10

The God Who's Already There

Have you ever decided to lose weight or stop smoking? We usually make such promises to ourselves each January, and by February we have already backslidden. New Year's resolutions seem to disappear faster than the morning fog on an East Texas pond. They start well enough but fade fast. So last year I gave up on making resolutions. Mine haven't been any more successful than most other people's. I still weigh about what I did thirty years ago, which has nothing to do with New Year's resolutions. I won't tell you the promises I have made to myself that I break every year, and I'm guessing your good intentions don't fare any better than mine.

Albert Einstein has been famously quoted as saying that the definition of insanity is to continue doing what we did before and expect a different result. So why do we keep doing it if we want to change?

I'm indebted to a friend of thirty years for a solution to this dilemma. James Surls is an artist. He's a big mountain of a man with the heart of a genuine romantic, both a pragmatist and a mystic. He works with his hands on large-scale pieces and with his heart on very expressive drawings. Recently he hung an impressive exhibit at the Gerald Peters Gallery, which happens to be right across the street from my office in Dallas.

I was hard at work one day when my assistant ducked around the corner to say, "You have a surprise visitor. James Surls is here." James had finished installing his show and had a little downtime just to hang out for a while. As I greeted him, I noted something was different about him. More on that in a second.

As we chatted like two old friends, James told me a story about one of his five daughters. He said, "You know one of my daughters is studying art at New York University. She called one day to ask, 'Dad, what is your manifesto?'" James replied, "Never thought about it. I don't have one." His daughter responded, "Well, Dad, one of my art professors has given me an assignment. He wants me to interview an artist to find out what his manifesto is, and you're it!"

"I thought about it for a minute," James said, "and three lines came to me." When James gave me the three, I was intrigued by what he said. I asked him if he would write them on a whiteboard in my office so that I could remember them and think about them. Here's what he wrote:

> Recognize the gift.
>
> Accept the gift.
>
> Execute the gift.

Those are great ideas for an artist and great for the rest

of us as well. Too often we focus on ourselves and miss the point of what truly forms our identities. The idea of a gift acknowledges that a very large part of what makes us who we are is from outside of us. It's not "I did this" or "I earned this," but "I received this. Whatever valuable talent, skill, or quality I have is a gift."

A good deal of humility is involved in accepting a gift. Whether a gift comes from God or from another person, it is something we possess but haven't earned. A gift is not an entitlement. A gift comes from the grace of the giver. A gift is not a transaction or an exchange. When you begin to think of your life as a collection of gifts, it takes the focus off yourself so that you can share the gift with the same generosity with which it was given. Life, then, is not a series of promises we make to ourselves that we cannot keep, but an adventure to share ourselves with others.

I am inspired by James's example. He has found the strength and humility to acknowledge the talent of "seeing" that has been granted him as a gift. He has the sense of responsibility and the work ethic to "execute the gift." I am his beneficiary, not only of the four pieces of his art that Linda and I live with every day, but of years of friendship and, even in an odd way, common cause. I have always known that there was something way beyond craft involved in James's sculptures and drawings, something transcendent, something symbolic.

Later in the day, Linda and I attended the opening reception for James's show. There, surrounded by a swirl of appreciative attendees and his work, James said, in his characteristically cryptic way of speaking, "You know I'm with you. I know where my gifts come from." He recognizes his gift. He accepts his gift. He acknowledges his Giver. And there, around us, were the evidences of the months of hard work with ax, welding torch, and pen that were the tangible results of his executing his gift. The title of the show was "Giving and Receiving"!

It's one thing to try and be a better person by periodically resolving to improve. There is nothing wrong with that. But maybe we need to spend more time recognizing the good that is already there and allowing it to blossom.

....

Reflection

1. What are your three greatest gifts — those talents, skills, abilities, or qualities that have been given to you?

2. At what point in your life did you begin to recognize those gifts?

3. Reflect on your gifts and ask yourself who encouraged or nurtured these gifts. A parent? A teacher? How could you do the same thing for someone else in your life?

4. How are you executing your gifts? How could you maximize your gifts for the benefit of others?

Wise Companions

The adventure of life is to learn.
The goal of life is to grow.
The nature of life is to change.
The challenge of life is to overcome.
The essence of life is to care.
The secret of life is to dare.
The beauty of life is to give.
The joy of life is to love.

WILLIAM ARTHUR WARD

A gift opens the way and ushers the giver into the presence of the great.

PROVERBS 18:16

When I consider your heavens,
    the work of your fingers,
the moon and the stars,
    which you have set in place,
what are mere mortals that you are mindful of them,
    human beings that you care for them?
You have made them a little lower than the heavenly
        beings
    and crowned them with glory and honor.

PSALM 8:3–5

CHAPTER 11

Giving for Results

Each year in its first issue, *Time* magazine features the "Person of the Year," an attempt to summarize — and pass judgment on — the most significant personality of the prior year. Linda and I have a tradition during the week between Christmas and New Year's Day of trying to guess who the featured person will be. In 2005 we were stumped because all the big media stories seemed to be wars and disasters: the war in Iraq; the tsunami in Indonesia; hurricanes Katrina, Rita, and Wilma in the United States. Would *Time* name an impersonal natural disaster?

A week later, in the January 2 issue of *Time*, it seemed to us that the editors made a perfect choice when they chose Bill and Melinda Gates and Bono as persons of the year. In so doing, they focused on results, not problems! The magazine's citation featured these lines of explanation: "Natural disasters are terrible things, but what ultimately defines us is not what happens to us, but how we react.... And who is proving more effective in figuring out how to eradicate those calamities? In different ways, it is Bill and Melinda Gates, co-founders of the world's wealthiest charitable foundation, and Bono, the Irish rocker who has made debt reduction sexy."

There is nothing particularly sexy about what I do, but my Buford Foundation letterhead these days has the heading "High Yield Philanthropy," which means I define the outcome of my daily engagements not by the process of giving away money, but by the *results* of the people the folks at Leadership Network and I invest our lives in. I intend to invest the results of my fortunate business experience, both what I learned and what I earned, in the mission that Peter Drucker defined so clearly for me in 1991 when he said, "Your work is to work on transforming the latent energy in American Christianity into active energy." Another phrase I heard over and over in virtually every conversation with Peter has shaped my thinking: "From good intentions to results and performance." Peter contended that most nonprofit organizations, almost all big foundations, and a good deal of government spending are invested in "good intentions." In his typically brusque style, he once told me, "Tell your rich friends money has no results. If money were what made the difference, Egypt would be Japan."

Peter wasn't speaking against money. He was simply saying that money alone won't get results. It might even impede results.

Reflecting on these "philanthropic superheroes," I began considering lessons I have learned from others that have become great motivations for generosity. We ordinary mortals, after all, certainly cannot imitate them in terms of either their wealth or fame, but that does not disqualify us from trying. These lessons will help you maximize your efforts to make the world a better place:

1. *Recognize the gift, accept the gift, execute the gift.* That's the manifesto that sculptor James Surls wrote on my whiteboard and which I described in the previous chapter. James has a remarkable ability to make art. He is also an encourager to many young, up-and-coming artists. I have been with him walking around an art colony near Snowmass, Colorado. He's a pied piper. So is Bono, who has used his influence for good to encourage the G8 countries to forgive poor nations some $40 billion in largely uncollectible debt. Rick Warren is doing much the same. His last email to me came from Rwanda. He was on his way to the World Economic Forum in Davos to encourage corporate titans to help those in poverty-stricken, war-torn African nations.

2. *Commit to personal engagement. Time* noted that Bill and Melinda Gates each spend fifteen hours a week in their philanthropic activities. Bill's father is involved in a virtually full-time leadership role. The whole family is hands-on staff. They travel. They see. They imagine what might be, just as Gates did when he imagined Microsoft. It's up close and personal, not distant and dispassionate.

3. *Focus on results.* Don't just figure out a process for giving. The objective is not to feel good personally or to relieve guilt by giving away money. Bill and Melinda Gates want to use their vision, compassion, and entrepreneurial ability to solve a problem, to achieve a highly specific

outcome. I have observed that people with excess capacity tend to ask one of two questions when someone is across the desk asking for their money: What's the least I can give this person and still feel okay in the morning? or, How much will it take to accomplish the outcome we're after?

Both the Gateses and Bono take a result-focused approach. The *Time* article noted that when considering a proposal to put computers in libraries, the Gateses asked, "Why not do them all?" Bono was not working the rich country leaders to reduce the debt burden on third world countries. He wanted to wipe the slate clean to give them a fresh start in life.

4. *Do it now.* There's an old expression I have heard several times recently. "I want to be givin' while I'm livin' so I'm knowin' where it's goin'." That's my approach, and it seems to be that of the Gateses as well. Give now and give it yourself. Don't dump the responsibility in the laps of the next generation. Jim Collins describes in his brilliant monograph, *Good to Great and the Social Sectors*, what he calls the Hedgehog Concept. He describes it this way: "to attain piercing clarity about how to produce the best long-term results and then to say 'no thank you' to opportunities that fail the Hedgehog test."[4] He describes the Hedgehog test in a diagram with three intersecting circles. If an opportunity does not fit within each of these circles, it fails the test and should be declined.

Passion is difficult to hire or to pass on to someone else years from now in a legal document setting up an "in perpetuity" foundation. Passion is personal. Passion is

What you are
deeply passionate
about.

What you can
be best in the
world at.

What drives
your resource
engine.

for now. Passion lapses if not put to work in a cause that ignites deep emotional engagement. The foundation I set up when I sold my company will be spent down in the next seven years to finance my passion. Peter Drucker was passionate about preserving our civilization through the medium of management. He told me once that the work he did to extend his legacy of ideas to the nonprofit world through the Drucker Foundation had added ten years to his life. Passion kept him alive!

5. *Consider a parallel career.* Similar to "Do it now," most all the people I see living for significance in their second half begin to allocate part of themselves much earlier in life. Bono is responsible to his band and his concert schedule, but everywhere he goes, he uses his celebrity and charisma to persuade presidents to help the world's poor about whom he cares deeply. Bill Gates still leads Microsoft. Rick Warren still leads Saddleback Church. All of

them have vigorous careers as social entrepreneurs along-side their "day jobs." If they can, so can the rest of us.

I know. I know. You're not a rock star. You haven't sold millions of books. You can't make art. But you and I can learn a lot from these world changers — a lot that can be applied to the up-close and personal situations that light us up. Give these lessons some thought, or better still, "Just do it!"

....

Reflection

1. What do you think Peter Drucker meant when he said, "Money has no results"? Do you agree? Why or why not?

2. Do you think generosity is easier for the wealthy? Why or why not? As your earnings have increased over the years, have you become more generous in terms of a percentage of your income?

3. What are you deeply passionate about? How does this passion influence your giving? How carefully do you monitor the results of your giving?

4. How personally involved are you in the causes you support?

5. What needs to be done for a cause you support that you are good at doing?

Wise Companions

He has shown all you people what is good.
    And what does the LORD require of you?
To act justly and to love mercy
    and to walk humbly with your God.

MICAH 6:8

If you don't break your ropes while you're alive,
Do you think ghosts will do it after?

KABIR (fourteenth-century Indian poet)

Make all you can, save all you can, give all you can.

JOHN WESLEY

We make a living by what we get; we make a life by
what we give.

WINSTON CHURCHILL

CHAPTER 12

Antidotes
to Aging Badly

E ach summer I try to schedule some study time in the mountain village of Aspen. During one of those invigorating retreats, I allocated some time to the subject of aging. It's the big demographic story of our time.

In that spirit, I chose to read *Everyman*, a novel by Pulitzer prize–winning author Philip Roth. It is the story of a seventy-one-year-old multidivorced, successful advertising executive facing the increasing frailty of old age. I found it to be the antitext on aging well. In this very well-written book, we see from the novelist's point of view — from inside the consciousness of a totally secularized Jewish man as he journeys through life and relationships. We experience *his* emotions. We live in *his* worldview. We enter into *his* relationships and *his* outcomes. We calculate with him *his* responses to others, *his* next moves.

I learned a good deal about myself by comparing how I might have approached his challenges with his responses to them. In fact, *Everyman* allowed me to see more clearly how I have actually approached the circumstances I have faced in my life — for example, how I have approached marriage, aging, and the temptations of "the world, the flesh, and the devil," to use the language of the *Book of Common Prayer*. How I process the events of my daily life; how I relate to God; how I look at the opportunities for significance that the second half of my life brings; and how I face the inevitability of death and what comes after. These comparisons caused me to develop a sort of *Cliffs-Notes on Aging*, a kind of checklist of the ideals I hope to live by as I age. Much more often than I would wish, I fall short of my aspirations, but at least I know what I'm trying to live up to. Believe me, it's a struggle.

Comparing black to white, darkness to light, silence to sound, intense fight or flight emotion to solitude and serenity, I learn a lot about both sides of these contrasts. White is whiter and brighter next to black.

In that spirit, I read Philip Roth's book and compared the *Everyman* approach to life with my own. See if any of the following comparisons resonate with your own situation.

Everyman	The Antidote
1. Exploitive selfish relationships that dry up over time.	Altruistic egoism. Ask everyone you encounter, "What can I do to be useful to you?" Train yourself in "otheration" as a habit. Earn your neighbors' love (Hans Selye).

Everyman	The Antidote
2. Cynical atheist. To die is to fall into an abyss of nothingness. All religions offend him. "There was only our bodies." His autobiography would be titled *The Life and Death of a Male Body* (p. 52).	Spend a lifetime building treasure in heaven. Visualize eternal life as Dante did, as hope for the future, as the best part of an abundant life. Self-transcendence.
3. Isolated from support systems, accountability, and team dynamics.	Long enduring relationships. Commitment to others. Relational equity in the "emotional bank account" of others. No investment = no return.
4. Health issues cause hyperfocus on the self, the body. It becomes the central, if not exclusive concern.	Engagement in helping others solve their problems.
5. Loss of purpose. No answer to "What now?"	Conceive a mission for yourself that honors God, serves God by serving others, and has visible benchmarks. Team building: a team, a coach, a small group. Vigorous engagement with a demanding project.
6. Loss of productivity.	Alignment with one's destiny and calling (self-transcendence). Do something that matters to others.

Everyman	The Antidote
7. Disease that finally kills him.	Preventive medicine. Diet habits and discipline. Exercise. Early diagnosis. Annual comprehensive physical — detect trouble early and fix it.
8. Lifelong preoccupation with death.	Accept that you don't know when. It's usually a surprise. Look forward to the eternal afterlife with a host of relationships that have gone before. Transcendence of this life in the next life.
9. Structureless retirement days with all old retired people who just dabble mindlessly. Move to retirement village at 65. "He had run out of interest in what he was doing" (p. 102).	Don't retire! Reposition. New routines and tastes appropriate to your current abilities and circumstances.
10. Loss of family by death or rejection by family due to prior hurts or just differing values. (Retired at age 65 after three divorces. Kids detested him. Wife: "You'll get no absolution from me — never!" [p. 123]).	"Adopt-a-parent" mentor (for me, Peter Drucker) whom you deeply respect. Be a friend to him. Soak his strength and insightfulness into your own life. Encourage others — especially those 20 to 30 years younger — to "adopt" someone your children's age who is receptive and with same values.

Everyman	The Antidote
11. Attempt to strain meaning out of a valueless hobby (painting in *Everyman*'s case) just to pass the time. Unrealistic, untested fantasy about what you will do in retirement. His kids called him "the happy cobbler" (p. 96).	Do something in which you are a primary supplier to a protected niche — a trusted adviser, a caregiver, a teacher. Either increase the activity or reduce the niche so that you are the go-to person.
12. Sexual temptation ("a desire that never lost its power to blind him and lead him") leading to lying and infidelity — destroying trust and credibility. Divorce, loss of children's respect. ("I did it for the worst possible reason: because I could," Bill Clinton.) You lose control of your life. Think "match point."	Appropriate boundaries. Don't start down a slippery slope. (Think *Fatal Attraction*, think *Medusa*.) Ask: Is it worth it? Appreciate what you have. Don't stretch beyond limits and boundaries.
13. Envy of his brother's health, wealth, purposefulness, family — "In his seventies, still vigorous and eager to be working" (p. 98). "In his old age, he had discovered the emotional state that robs the envier of his serenity and, worse, his realism" (p. 101).	Build on your own islands of health and strength, on your own purpose and destiny.

Everyman	The Antidote
14. Living in a memoryland of reminiscence because there is no present and no imaginable hope for the future. He is trapped in his ailing body. He was "looking hungrily back at the superabundant past" (p. 102).	A new purpose, a new task for a new season. Think "Ulysses," by Tennyson. Think Peter Drucker, Frances Hesselbein, Pablo Cassals, Brendan Gill, Brooke Astor.
15. Loss of confidence, loneliness. Hesitancy to reach out to others, loss of satisfying contact. "The vitriolic despondency of one once assertively in the middle of everything who was now in the middle of nothing.... Lost and drifting, the dread began to seep in" (p. 103).	Do things that matter to someone even if they are "little things." Stay engaged in satisfying someone else's need. Stay combative. "Do not go gentle into that dark night. Rage, rage" (Dylan Thomas).
16. Stagnation, hollowness, isolation, displaced, uprooted. "He had displaced himself just when age most demanded that he be rooted for all those years he ran the creative department at the agency. This was stagnation ... barrenness ... a sense of otherness" (p. 129).	Focus on the positives. Keep a Book of Days. Make a list each week of positive contributions to the lives of others. Count your blessings and multiply them.

Everyman	The Antidote
17. Loss of interest in everything. "He explained to Nancy that he'd had an irreversible aesthetic vasectomy." "Nothing any longer kindled his curiosity" (p. 138).	Stay creative and creating. Think Henri Matisse, Pablo Picasso, Beethoven. Take on a new learning agenda.
18. Overwhelmed by regrets and a plague of "if onlys" (pp. 107–8).	Do the right thing in the first place. When you err, seek forgiveness: from God (grace) and from others you have hurt. Think AA 12 Steps.
19. A rush of bad news about the health of same-age friends, family, colleagues. About his ex-wife: "Her beauty, frail to begin with, was smashed and broken. She looked shrunken and already on the way to decomposing" (p. 139).	Stay engaged in projects with younger people. Serve them. Make yourself useful. (The counterexample in Roth's book is the head of his ad agency, Clarence Spraco, who was engaged to the end at age 84; pp. 142–48).
20. "Self-admonition, insufficiency, assailed by remorse, aimless days, waiting and waiting for nothing. He would have to continue to manage alone, foreboding of helplessness to come" (pp. 158–62).	Comparison case: Peter Drucker, who worked writing and helping others into his 90s. His last *WSJ* article was when he was 94. Three weeks before he died, he said to his wife of 60 years, "I don't think I will write anymore." He lapsed into a coma during which he repeatedly said the Lord's Prayer in German. Then he died.

Everyman	The Antidote
21. Everyman died in surgery, destitute of faith and friends at age 71. "He listened to the rabbi and nodded his head, but he did not number himself among the believers, let alone the observant" (p. 167).	Comparison case: Czeslaw Milosz, the Nobel Prize–winning poet (1980) returned late in life to his native Poland. He died in 2004 in Krakow. "Late Ripeness" (see Wise Companions) was among his last poems.

I'm thankful for novelists like Philip Roth who don't try to sugarcoat their view of life with contrived plots and happy endings. I learn more about myself when I read a book like this than I do when I read a book with all the "answers." Answers were more important to me in my first half. The second half is a time for asking honest questions and being willing to face the answers. The reality is that we will not live forever — not in this world at least. Yet aging should never be feared or ignored.

Live well; age gracefully.

Reflection

1. When you were in your twenties, what did you think about the age you are now? How do you feel about that age now? What has changed?

2. Most of our culture's antidotes to aging focus on the external: hair coloring or replacements, surgery to eliminate wrinkles and "repackage" our bodies, salves and lotions to rejuvenate our skin and erase age spots. What are some internal antidotes to aging that you can use to "stay young"?

3. What do you fear about growing older? What do you look forward to as you grow older?

4. What is it about retirement that is so appealing? How do you respond to my admonition to "never retire"?

5. Think about someone you know who is "really old" yet defies all descriptions of old age. What is it about that person that you admire? What qualities does he or she model that you would like to emulate?

Wise Companions

Late Ripeness

Not soon, as late as the approach of my ninetieth year,
I felt a door opening in me and I entered
the clarity of early morning.
One after another my former lives were departing,
like ships, together with their sorrow.
And the countries, cities, gardens, the bays of seas
assigned to my brush came closer,
ready now to be described better than they were before.
I was not separated from people,
grief and pity joined us.
We forget — I kept saying — that we are all children of the
*   King.*
For where we come from there is no division
into Yes and No, into is, was, and will be.
We were miserable, we used no more than a hundredth part
of the gift we received for our long journey.
Moments from yesterday and from centuries ago —
a sword blow, the painting of eyelashes before a mirror
of polished metal, a lethal musket shot, a carvel
staving its hull against a reef — they dwell in us,
waiting for a fulfillment.
I knew, always, that I would be a worker in the vineyard,
as are all men and women living at the same time,
whether they are aware of it or not.

CZESLAW MILOSZ[5]

But I have raised you up for this very purpose, that I might show you my power and that my name might be proclaimed in all the earth.

Exodus 9:16

O God, thou hast made us for thyself, and our hearts are restless until they find rest in thee.

Augustine

CHAPTER 13

The Paradox of Power

In the major transitions of my life, I have given up a certain level of power in order to move on to the next thing. When I handed the leadership of my company over to others, I also handed over the power to make strategic decisions. Recently I moved the offices for my foundation out of the office suite for Leadership Network, the organization I started to carry out my second-half mission. It was a symbolic move, but symbolism is important. For the first time, the two organizations are no longer connected by a common hallway. I can go see them. They can come see me. But we don't run into one another at the water cooler anymore. I still do plenty of things with them, but once again, I gave up some of my power in this transition.

In *Halftime*, I used Charles Handy's illustration of the Sigmoid Curve to illustrate this change-of-season phenomenon. Handy, author of *The Age of Paradox*, says, "It is one of the paradoxes of success that the things and ways which got you there are seldom those that keep you there."[6]

Handy offers a solution: The secret to constant growth is to start a new Sigmoid Curve before the first one loses steam. The right place to start that second curve is at Point A (see the diagram below), where there is the time, as well as the resources and energy, to get the new curve through its initial explorations and flounderings before the first curve begins to dip downward.

THE SIGMOID CURVE
by Charlies Handy, *The Age of Paradox*

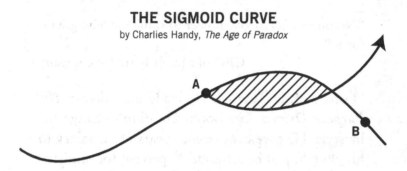

Tom Luce, who left the Leadership Network board to be the U.S. assistant secretary of education, says my greatest challenge is going to be "letting go," which directly applies to the subject of power. Tom's wise counsel has been much on my mind as I wrestle with the issue of power. We may not admit it, but all of us want power — the power to influence others, the power to get our phone calls returned, the power to get things done that are important to us.

I meet for breakfast with a small group of men each month in a high-rise club overlooking Dallas. Last month's discussion, led by a well-known money manager, was about power. Our leader set it up this way: "Recently, in counseling with a young man, I concluded that his greatest goal was to have power. At the end of our meeting, I told him that power was a by-product of effort, skill, energy, and time. I further stated that you don't 'just decide' to be powerful. Was I correct?"

A lively discussion began. I took notes as fast as I could. Here is what I heard:

"No one wants to give power to someone who grasps for it."

CEO of a publicly traded company

"Look at Rick Warren. He made millions on *The Purpose-Driven Life* book. He didn't change his lifestyle. He gave back twenty years of his salary to his church, and he set aside 90 percent for ministry projects like AIDS in Africa. He might be the most powerful guy in U.S. Christianity today. He gained power by giving it away."

PHILANTHROPIST

"Look at Mother Teresa, Martin Luther King, and Gandhi."

ENTREPRENEUR

"Bob Strauss once told me about power: 'If you ever have to use it, you just lost it.'"

ATTORNEY quoting the legendary
Washington power broker

"You get more of it by giving it away."

THE CEO

"I have always thought it was very fortunate that being a good steward was also good business."

THE MONEY MANAGER

Most of us seemed to feel that power is paradoxical, that it flees from those who grasp for it and accrues to those who surrender it in the service of their mission on earth. As Frances Hesselbein, an authority on leadership, told me when I interviewed her for my book *Finishing Well*, "I have a very strong belief that we are called to do what we do, and when we're called, we're given the energy. And when we're no longer called, we will not have the energy."

As for me, I have decided that just about all that will be left of me when I leave this earth is what I can let go of to invest in the lives of others. The fruit of my life and my work will grow up on other people's trees. It's not easy to do. It's a paradox, but sixty-six years of life so far demonstrate to me that it works.

Reflection

1. Identify everyone over whom you have some level of power or authority — at work, in your family, at church, in your community. How have you obtained that power? How do you use it? Is power something you enjoy, or do you find yourself uncomfortable with it?

2. Have you experienced a change or transition in your life that led you to give up some of your power? How did you feel about that? Was it difficult? Do you find yourself still trying to exercise that power?

3. The "big three" temptations for most successful people are money, fame, and power. Which one are you most vulnerable to? Why? What are you doing to protect yourself from that temptation?

4. As you contemplate the transition from success to significance, what will you gain from letting go of the power you now have?

Wise Companions

Next Jesus was taken into the wild by the Spirit for the Test. The Devil was ready to give it. Jesus prepared for the Test by fasting forty days and forty nights....

For the third test, the Devil took him to the peak of a huge mountain. He gestured expansively, pointing out all the earth's kingdoms, how glorious they all were. Then he said, "They're yours — lock, stock, and barrel. Just go down on your knees and worship me, and they're yours."

Jesus' refusal was curt: "Beat it, Satan!" He backed his rebuke with a third quotation from Deuteronomy: "Worship the Lord your God, and only him. Serve him with absolute single-heartedness."

The Test was over. The Devil left. And in his place, angels! Angels came and took care of Jesus' needs.

MATTHEW 4:1, 8–11 MSG

For God's sake, let us sit upon the ground
And tell sad stories of the death of kings:
How some have been depos'd; some slain in war;
Some haunted by the ghosts they have depos'd;
Some poison'd by their wives; some sleeping kill'd;
All murder'd: for within the hollow crown
That rounds the mortal temples of a king
Keeps Death his court, and there the antick sits,
Scoffing his state and grinning at his pomp,
Allowing him a breath, a little scene,
To monarchize, be fear'd and kill with looks,
Infusing him with self and vain conceit
As if this flesh which walls about our life
Were brass impregnable, and humour'd thus
Comes at the last and with a little pin
Bores through his castle wall, and farewell king!
        WILLIAM SHAKESPEARE, *King Richard II*

CHAPTER 14

Prayer as a State of Being

I will begin with a parable by Leo Tolstoy that gets to the heart of prayer. It is quoted in *Spiritual Direction*, a book by my friend the late Henri Nouwen.

"Three Monks on an Island"

Three Russian monks lived on a faraway island. Nobody ever went there, but one day their bishop decided to make a pastoral visit. When he arrived, he discovered that the monks didn't even know the Lord's Prayer. So he spent all his time and energy teaching them the "Our Father" and then left, satisfied with his pastoral work. But when his ship had left the island and was back in the open sea, he suddenly noticed the three hermits walking on the water — in fact, they were running after the ship! When they reached it, they cried, "Dear Father, we have forgotten the prayer you taught us."

The bishop, overwhelmed by what he was seeing and hearing, said, "But, dear brothers, how then do you pray?" They answered, "Well, we just say, 'Dear God, there are three of us and there are three of you, have mercy on us!'" The bishop, awestruck by their sanctity and simplicity, said, "Go back to your land and be at peace."

Henri follows this parable by saying, "There's a difference between *reciting* prayers and *prayerfulness*."[7]

The apostle Paul taught that we should "pray continually," or as the King James Version says, "without ceasing" (1 Thess. 5:17). On the surface, that seems like one of those impossible exhortations from Scripture, but I think that what he meant is that true prayer is not separate from daily life. It is a way of being. For me, it is like being with Linda for a weekend at the farm. We're just there with one another. We talk over lunch and dinner, but it doesn't particularly matter what we say. It is more about who we are. It is about being together, sharing life with someone you love and trust. Prayer is a state of being together with God. It is not necessarily triggered by liturgy or special needs.

To be sure, there is a place for reciting familiar prayers. I say the Lord's Prayer, the Doxology, and other liturgical prayers seldom in the day but often at night. When I wake up from sleep, I have a tendency to role-play my coming day in imagination, especially if I am anxious about the day ahead. Giving a speech. Confronting something that's not going especially well. Once I get that kind of thought going, I have difficulty getting back to sleep. So I fill the void with ritual prayer. If I have been with an especially stimulating, emotionally engaging group of people the day before, I find that they stay in my head at night. They're still there. If they have strong personalities, they leave emotional impressions. I'm still doing business with them, saying things we didn't say, finishing conversations we didn't complete — wondering if there is more we will say or do. Knowing that there is only so much room in the mental box, I "sing" silently the Doxology or repeat the Lord's Prayer, often drifting back into sleep knowing that I am loved by God, a love that fills the God-shaped void within me.

Often when I pray, I use a framework that has come echoing down century after century. It's easy to remember using the acronym ACTS, which stands for:

Adoration
Confession
Thanksgiving
Supplication

Adoration. Adoration means being mindful of God's characteristics. Sometimes it helps to use a praise song or a psalm like this one:

O LORD, You have searched me and known me.
You know my sitting down and my rising up;
You understand my thought afar off.
You comprehend my path and my lying down,
And are acquainted with all my ways.

Psalm 139:1–3 NKJV

Confession. My own confessions typically concern my childish and natural self-absorption. I ask for and receive forgiveness.

Thanksgiving. I spend most of my prayer time these days expressing thanks. Often I use a mechanism I learned from psychologist Larry Crabb in his appropriately titled book *Inside Out.* Imagine a target that looks like the following:

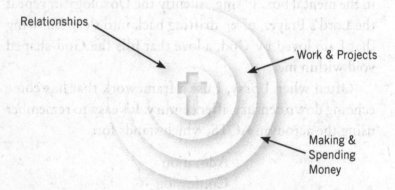

I begin in the center of the target and pray my way outward. First, I express gratitude for what Christ has done for me — for my life now and my eternal life to come. I move on to the relationships I'm grateful for, then to projects I've had the privilege to work on with others. And last, I'm thankful for the material treasures that are a platform for my life and work.

Supplication. In supplication we ask for what we need. Lately this is always the shortest section, where I often just say the phrase, "Thy will be done on earth (and in my life) as it is in heaven." I have always felt this is the most perfect prayer we can pray.

Sometimes, particularly when I'm driving (eyes open!) or walking alone for exercise, I use my hands as aids to prayer. I hold a hand upward for praise, palm forward for confession, imagining that my palm rests on the chest of Christ on the cross, my sins transferring to him. For thanksgiving I turn my palm up in an attitude of receiving; and for supplication I turn my palm down, leaving my concerns in the lap of God.

I always feel renewed and refreshed in the knowledge that while things seldom turn out as I have planned and imagined them, they always seem to turn out. Is it me? Is it God intervening? Is it the interaction of my wishes with those of hundreds of other people who have their own wishes? I don't know, and I don't need to know. We live in a mystery. Each of us stares into a reality others can't see. We must not presume to know too much.

This I know: there is a God. And he is not distant, but close at hand. He is part of me, braided into who I am. I'm never alone. He loves me. I trust him.

In his book *Praying Like Jesus*, author James Mulholland confesses that when he prayed as a child, his prayers were said mostly to please his parents as he dutifully said grace before meals and "Now I lay me down to sleep" at night. "Many of our first prayers are prayed to please others," he wrote.[8] Sometimes we still pray to please others, yet if we allow prayer to become an attitude instead of a duty or a badge of spirituality, we will discover that God is truly with us. Right now. Forever.

Reflection

1. If you had only three words, how would you describe your relationship with God? Is it *personal*, *intimate*, *distant*, *trusting*, *suspicious*? How is it?

2. When do you feel closest to God? Is it a special time or place? Or anyplace?

3. Does God speak to you? When you ring, does he answer? How? Through the Word? Through intuition? Through imagination — you "just know"? Through people? Through circumstances?

4. Do you believe it is possible to "pray without ceasing"? How can you move from "saying prayers" to developing an attitude of prayer?

5. Do unanswered prayers trouble you? How do you reconcile the idea that God is always with you and for you yet sometimes your prayers are not answered?

Wise Companions

It is a matter of great skill to know how to converse with Jesus; and to know how to keep Jesus, a point of great wisdom. Be thou humble and peaceable, and Jesus will be with thee. Be devout and quiet, and Jesus will stay with thee.

THOMAS À KEMPIS

For it is fitting for the master to speak and to teach, but the disciple should be silent and listen.

SAINT BENEDICT

My father wasn't in the delivery room or even in the building; the halls of Wilson Hospital were close and short, and Dad had gone out to pace in the damp September wind. He was praying, rounding the block for the fifth time, when the air quickened. He opened his eyes and discovered he was running — sprinting across the grass toward the door.

"How'd you know?" I adored this story, made him tell it all the time.

"God told me you were in trouble."

"Out loud? Did you hear Him?

"Nope, not out loud. But he made me run, Reuben. I guess I figured it out on the way."

LEIF ENGER, *Peace Like a River*

CHAPTER 15

Born Again and Again— An Easter Reflection

I have never been one to use the words "born again" to describe the gift of faith. I have nothing in particular against this familiar and fitting metaphor. I just don't recall ever describing myself as a "born-again" Christian. Rather than thinking of being born again as a single experience, I believe we are called to rebirth again and again — maybe not to belief but in discovering what to do with what we believe. *Halftime* is the beginning of multiple "new beginnings," a mind-set of expectation in which new ideas, new challenges, and new opportunities are the norm.

I am writing this shortly after awakening at five in the morning, fresh as a flower after a good night's sleep and looking forward to a new springtime in my life and work. I have plenty of great, new things to pour myself into the next ten years, and for that I am grateful. The sun splashes across the Dallas landscape. I hear the hum of traffic waking up on the streets nineteen floors below and the morning's first jet rising up from Love Field as all the commercial energy of the city comes alive for a new day.

Every day gives us a chance to experience a life reborn in the spirit of Easter — invigorating eagerness to rise above a world grown tired of cynicism and gridlock. Let's get up and go do something about it!

There is brand-new passion in my sixtysomething friends, the pathfinders of the new demographic season, the Second Half. Real estate magnate Don Williams is bubbling over with new energy to champion an "extreme makeover" of the Dallas Independent School District that will bring new opportunities for poor kids. Former colleague and now U.S. assistant secretary of education Tom Luce is championing a revised season of No Child Left Behind with Ted Kennedy on his side — finally, something out of Washington that's bi-partisan. And bestselling author Ken Blanchard has a recent $5 million injection of capital for his new endeavor, Lead Like Jesus. He says, "Leadership is primarily about two things: results and relationships." All of these men could have retired very comfortably five years ago.

Several weeks ago I heard that the Gates Foundation had received *1,000 downloads* of capital from foundations around the country, inspired by Warren Buffett's having committed his $42 billion to Bill and Melinda Gates. It's an innovative approach for philanthropy that has captivated Buffet, who is in a new season of his life at age seventy-eight. Rick Warren is working tirelessly to alleviate AIDS in Africa and doing other things that build on the unique character and enthusiasm of faith-based organizations.

You could say that these men are being born again and again and again.

By the way of counterpoint, I recall what Henri Nouwen did in his sixties. After often being hailed as the successor to Thomas Merton and having a one-of-a-kind career as superstar teacher-priest at Notre Dame, Yale, and Harvard, he — perhaps one of the most gregarious people I've known — retreated to L'Arche in Toronto to be a caregiver to just one mentally challenged individual. Henri is now in heaven. Does God honor his halftime decision to live a new life, moving from success to significance to surrender (his words) more or less than the others I have named? I wonder.

I left behind the wonderful adventure of running my business and acquiring wealth because I believed that the best was ahead of me. This morning of this day, like so many days before, it is proving to be true. I am becoming born again, again. And I'm just getting started!

Reflection

1. What is it that gives you energy as opposed to depleting your energy? For example, some people gain energy from being with people; others are more likely to get a rush of energy from solitude. How can you program more energy-building experiences into your life on a more consistent basis?

2. What changes in your life are you embracing and celebrating? What changes in your life are you resisting or dreading? Why?

3. What would a rebirth, a new season, a fresh beginning look like for you? In other words, if you could "start over," what would you do?

4. What cause, mission, or adventure is worth betting the next ten years of your life on?

Wise Companions

Thus says God the LORD,
Who created the heavens
  and stretched them out,
Who spread forth the earth
  and that which comes from it,
Who gives breath to the people on it,
And spirit to those who walk on it: ...
"Behold, the former things have come to pass,
And new things I declare;
Before they spring forth
  I tell you of them."
Sing to the LORD a new song, ...
"I, even I, am He who blots out
  your transgressions for My own sake;
And I will not remember your sins....
Behold, I will do a new thing,
Now it shall spring forth;
Shall you not know it?"

  ISAIAH 42:5, 9–10; 43:25, 19 NKJV

Lives of great men all remind us
We can make our lives sublime,
And, departing, leave behind us
Footprints in the sands of time.

  HENRY WADSWORTH LONGFELLOW,
  "A Song of Life"

CHAPTER 16

Reviewing Grace

I have never written a film review, but I'm compelled to do so now. If you haven't seen it, I'm recommending that you rent my new favorite halftime movie. The story takes place in a different time and in a different nation, but it couldn't be more inspiring and on target for anyone on the journey from success to significance. If you need encouragement to stay on the path you've chosen, you will get it in large doses with this movie.

Amazing Grace is based on the life of one of the greatest halftime true stories ever lived, that of antislavery pioneer William Wilberforce. The film's star, Ioan Gruffudd, superbly embodies Wilberforce who, as a member of Parliament, navigated the world of eighteenth-century backroom politics to end the slave trade in the British Empire. Albert Finney plays John Newton, a reformed slave ship owner and a confidant of Wilberforce who inspires him to pursue a life of service to humanity (Newton penned the hymn "Amazing Grace," thus the title of the movie). Benedict Cumberbatch plays William Pitt the Younger who, at twenty-four, was England's youngest ever prime minister. Pitt encourages Wilberforce to take up the fight to outlaw slavery and supports him in his struggles in Parliament. When Wilberforce at one point considers becoming a clergyman as a way to live out his deep faith, Pitt challenges him, saying, "Would you rather praise the Lord or change the world?"

Over the course of two decades, Wilberforce takes on the English establishment and persuades those in power to end the inhumane slave trade at huge cost to their business enterprises. At the time, asking plantation owners to do without slave labor was something like asking today's multinational corporations to operate without petroleum.

Wilberforce sees the end of the British slave trade in 1807 when Parliament passes his abolition bill by a large majority. Twenty-six years later, just three days before his death, slavery is abolished in all British colonies as well. Talk about significance! And, of course, British abolition had a profound effect on the conflict over slavery that led to the American Civil War.

Author and abolitionist Harriet Beecher Stowe praised Wilberforce in the pages of *Uncle Tom's Cabin*. Novelist E. M. Forster compared him to Gandhi. Abraham Lincoln invoked his memory in a celebrated speech. In the houses of South Africa's parliament, Nelson Mandela recalled Wilberforce's tireless labor on behalf of the sons and daughters of Africa, calling Britain "the land of William Wilberforce — who dared to stand up to demand that the slaves in our country should be freed." Nevertheless, Wilberforce is barely known in the United States today.

Why am I recommending a film that came and went

with little box office success? Because I know there will be times when you doubt that what you are doing is of real significance. Heroic films like *Amazing Grace* inspire us. We secretly covet the hero's role and imagine ourselves standing up for what is right regardless of the cost. Your decision to buck the trend and shift your attention to a higher calling is no less important than Wilberforce's tireless and oft-thwarted efforts to end slavery. If I am successful in my mission to unlock the latent energy in the church, the world could be changed. And if you stick with your mission, I am convinced you will experience the same satisfaction Wilberforce felt three days before he died — and yes, we both may have to wait that long. But it will be worth it.

I also recommend this movie because I have chosen to be *for* people and movements that build better lives rather than spending my energy crying out *against* the darkness of our times. As you discover and refine your own mission, consider the following three guidelines:

1. Build on the islands of health and strength.
2. Work only with those who are receptive to what you are trying to do and with what is trying to be born.
3. Work on things that have a multiplier effect ("hundredfold yield").

Now for one of those amazing ironies I keep bumping into. The risk capital and the visionary influence behind

Amazing Grace comes from my friend Phil Anschutz, who has chosen a second-half parallel career of making high-quality films with redemptive themes (e.g., *Ray* and *The Lion, the Witch and the Wardrobe*). I wasn't thinking of Phil when I jumped into my own halftime, but you never know what will happen when you listen to your inner calling. I celebrate Phil's courage, commitment, and countercultural instinct. Knowing that he is ever modest, low-key, and press shy, I asked Phil if I could use his name in this review. His response: "Bob, it is okay for you to use my name on this one, but please don't overdo it! I'm just a normal guy following your precept of working on things that count (i.e., 100X)."

As you pursue your second-half mission, there will be times when you wonder if you have set your sights too high. Whenever you feel that way, download the movie *Amazing Grace*.

Reflection

1. What have you already done, even in a small way, that was heroic?

2. Wilberforce faced enormous barriers but never gave up. Who or what is standing in your way, and what motivates you to keep going?

3. What are the two or three guiding principles for the things and people in which you are willing to invest your resources?

4. Who can you be "for" as opposed to what you could be against?

5. If you accomplish your second-half mission, who will it benefit and how?

Wise Companions

Permanence, perseverance, and persistence in spite of all obstacles, discouragements, and impossibilities: It is this that in all things distinguishes the strong soul from the weak.

SIR FRANCIS DRAKE

Work is the grand cure of all the maladies and miseries that ever beset mankind.

THOMAS CARLYLE

Life begets life.
Energy becomes energy.
It is by spending oneself
that one becomes rich.

SARAH BARNHARDT

Faith without works is dead.... Be doers of the word, and not hearers only, deceiving yourselves.

JAMES 2:20; 1:22 NKJV

Do one thing everyday that scares you.

ELEANOR ROOSEVELT

CHAPTER 17

The More You Have, the Harder It Is to Give It Away

Do you believe it is more blessed to give than to receive? Do you *really* believe it? I do. I have attempted to develop a life around this idea, and my experience proves it is true — giving is infinitely better than receiving.

Then why is it so difficult for me and for others to give?

Warren Buffett, whose $42 billion gift to the Bill and Melinda Gates Foundation in 2006[9] positions him as an expert on the subject of giving (as well as getting) money, said during his announcement that making money can be a lot easier than successfully giving it away.

Every spring *Forbes* magazine publishes a list of the world's richest people. There are now 891 billionaires in the United States.[10]

The year 2005 was a good year for billionaires. Two-thirds of them became richer than they were the preceding year. And this was *after* their charitable giving and *after* any part of their fortunes had been transferred to family members. The average age of U.S. billionaires is sixty-two, and 60 percent made their fortunes from scratch. These fortunes just grow and grow.

You would think that, having so much excess, these wealthy people would give a higher proportion of their net worth than those with less. Studies on giving behavior show mixed outcomes, but it is not at all certain that the rich give a larger percentage of their annual income than do those in lower income brackets. They certainly give less when the measure is a percentage of net worth.

For years I have puzzled about why this is so. Almost twenty years ago I attended a by-invitation-only conference in Bermuda for well-off Christians. During a sun-splashed breakfast on the terrace of a luxury hotel, I asked Harvard psychiatrist Dr. Armand Nicholi why rich people, knowing they won't live forever and that their families are bountifully provided for, don't give away more of their excess. Armand is a profound and careful thinker, so I expected "the big answer." I was stunned when he said, "I guess they are just selfish." I am not convinced he's right. Surely it's more than selfishness that prevents the wealthy from being more generous.

From my own experience and observing others, the reason it is so hard for wealthy people to give a higher percentage of their net worth is tied to risk — not so much monetary risk as ego risk. Here are the three big risks philanthropists face: fear, failure, and harm.

Fear. As improbable as it may sound, I know people whose nest eggs are enough to cover every contingency for the rest of their lives, yet they hold back "just in case" a reversal of fortune occurs. They could easily give back several times more then they do each year without the slightest risk to themselves. Their lives are less rich for holding back. Mother Teresa called this "the poverty of the rich."

Failure. In his book *The Foundation*, Joel Fleishman glowingly subtitles his volume, *A Great American Secret; How Private Wealth Is Changing the World.* In addition to reporting on private philanthropy's success, he describes some notorious failures. For example, publishing baron Walter Annenberg donated $500 million to improve the quality of America's public schools, yet it is generally agreed that the impact was negligible.[11]

Giving money away successfully requires a very different skill set than making money, for which we generally launch the right business at the right time and let the score run up. For some entrepreneurs, making money almost comes naturally, yet it seems that more is never enough. But every gift has to overcome the force of gravity. Every gift is a small triumph of self-denial over self-interest, especially if one hasn't, through practice, acquired the habit. However, no one wants to give away his or her money and discover it did little good. So the alternative is to give away very little: small investment, small failure.

Harm. If fear of failure is one risk, fear of actually doing more harm than good keeps a lot of money in the pockets of the wealthy. Bill Damon, a senior fellow at the Hoover Institution, has written widely on ethical and moral commitment. Here's what he says in his 2006 book, *Taking Philanthropy Seriously*:

Andrew Carnegie, founder of organized philanthropy in the United States, once estimated that 95 percent of philanthropic dollars were "unwisely spent; so spent, indeed, as to produce the very evils which [the giver] proposes to mitigate or cure."

It is unfortunately the case that the act of giving is also not always able to improve the lot of those it is intended to help. More unfortunate still, the benevolence of philanthropy can manage at times to worsen the conditions of the intended beneficiaries. Perhaps most astonishing of all, the gift of money is not always sufficient to win even the gratitude of those who get it.

In our discussions with grantees who regularly receive philanthropic funds, we found many complaints and few accolades. Recipients rarely felt that they had been treated with respect. They felt that their efforts had been undermined by restrictions or requirements imposed on them as a condition of support.... Perhaps they resented the hoops they were forced to jump through in order to garner support for their cherished causes.[12]

I know this sounds negative, but based on my experience, these three risks are real. It's certainly more comfortable just to keep the money, but there is a dark side to not giving as well. In addition to actual financial loss, other kinds of losses occur when we don't exploit an opportunity. Not following one's destiny falls in this category. This risk is what likely drives Bill and Melinda Gates to attempt to cure disease in Africa. They might fail, but the greater risk is to fail to try.

Andrew Carnegie wrote of opportunity loss when he resolved at age thirty-three to reinvest himself (not just his money) in "education and the improvement of the poorer classes." He wrote in his journal:

> Man must have an idol — the amassing of wealth is one of the worst species of idolatry. No idol more debasing than the worship of money. Whatever I engage in I must push inordinately; therefore I should be careful to choose that life which will be the most elevating in its character. To continue much longer overwhelmed by business cares and with most of my thoughts wholly upon the way to make more money in the shortest time, must degrade me beyond hope of permanent recovery.[13]

Carnegie gave away 90 percent of his fortune in his lifetime. He had a wonderful life doing it. He traded money for meaning.

You most likely are not in the same league as an Andrew Carnegie or a Warren Buffet, yet the concept remains true: the more you have, the more difficult it is to give. It only becomes easier when you understand what you lose by holding on to your wealth and what you gain by letting your passion — your calling — have prominence over your money.

Reflection

1. Spend some time informally analyzing your current financial position. Your net worth. Liquidity. Debt. Rate your sense of financial security on a scale of 1 to 10, with 10 being, "If I stopped whatever I'm doing to earn more money, I could live very comfortably for the rest of my life."

2. What percentage of your net worth do you typically give to charitable causes each year? What prevents you from giving more? Of the three "risks" outlined in this chapter — fear, failure, harm — which pertains most to you?

3. What motivates your giving? Is it focused on a single cause or calling? Do you give out of a sense of obligation? Are you intimately involved with the recipients of your giving?

4. Recall one of your most recent significant donations. What did you gain from your gift? What did you lose?

5. If you could align your deepest passion with your charitable giving, how would that change the way you donated your money?

Wise Companions

Money has materialized the church. The money she does not give has earthened her. Money-loving, money-making, money-keeping is the rock on which the spiritual movements of the church are stranded.

E. M. BOUNDS

Charity is such a wise merchant that she always makes a profit where others lose, and she always escapes the fetters with which others are bound, and so she has a great quantity of things that are pleasing to Love.

MARGUERITE PORETE,
a thirteenth-century woman burned
at the stake for the ideas in her book
The Mirror of Simple Souls

CHAPTER 18

Do Less
to Get More Done

Ken and Margie Blanchard are experts in teaching and learning. Ken has now coauthored forty books with others. They are short books with big lessons, the most popular being *The One Minute Manager*. Margie leads the Blanchard Training Company's "Office of the Future." Ken calls himself the chief spiritual officer of that enterprise. We are on the boards of one another's "significance" enterprises.

Ken's preeminent frustration in life is the knowing-doing gap. People read his books by the millions and attend his seminars by the thousands. Ken's aggravation is that only a small percentage of them do what they learn they should do. When people praise his work, he sometimes asks them, "How has knowing that changed the way you behave?" He says that "most people have a hard time answering that question. They often change the subject by talking about another concept or some other work they are reading."

Like most of these people, I, a self-professed pack rat, accumulator of random bits of information, and serial processor of emails, conversation, and magazine articles, do just what Ken is talking about. I fail to carry out my good intentions. Other people sometimes feed my habit. Dave Travis, who heads our Church Innovation Team at Leadership Network, recently emailed me his own sixty-two page collection of recent readings. Meanwhile, piles of unread books and magazines stack up at the farm.

This week I got overwhelmed. I'm working on several new ventures at once — most leaping forward, some lagging. I was trying to scatter some effort here and some there to make incremental progress, and it was just too much. My mind was numb, and while trying to do three things at once, I was essentially going around in circles. It was like the opening lines of Keats's famous poem, "Ode to a Nightingale."

> *My heart aches, and a drowsy numbness pains*
> *My sense, as though of hemlock I had drunk,*
> *Or emptied some dull opiate to the drains.*

No kidding. It was like that for a few hours. It was like walking in mud. Does that ever happen to you?

Thank God, help was on the way. Ken had slipped one of his books into my backpack when I saw him in Chicago recently. It popped to the surface and cleared a lot of this mental underbrush up in less than an hour.

In *Know Can Do!* he and his two coauthors describe what they call "information overload" — basically we overdose ourselves on knowledge and it immobilizes us. It's what some people call "paralysis by analysis."

Ken explains it: "This is the common trap to fall into

because it is easy to read a new book, listen to a new CD or go to a seminar. Knowledge comes easy, but that will not bring about a change of behavior.... At the end of a book, people will have less than five percent recall of material they are exposed to. It's more fun to find out something new than to struggle to use what you know."[14]

What's the fix to closing the knowing-doing gap? Ken says, "We have to decide what we need to learn to help us live better and then go about it with vigor." Or to put it in a Blanchard-esque formula: "People should learn *less* more and not *more* less."[15]

The logical corollary for me is to do less in order to get more done. Long before he ran for president in the 1990s, Texas billionaire Ross Perot had a reputation for succeeding at everything he did. I once asked my friend Tom Luce, who knew Perot, what he considered the key to Perot's success. Tom said it simply: "He can focus."

Can you resolve to be more focused and to "learn less more"? Resolving to do that is one thing; doing it is another. I'm going to try, and I'll start by disposing of some of my stacks of "I'll read it someday when I have time" material at the farm. Then I'm going to take a nap. Or take a brisk walk on a country road. I'm going to listen to "the still, small voice" and try to reconnect with the God who has always been there for me. I'm going to abandon a couple of bright ideas that haven't worked in order to focus on the islands of health and strength in the zones I feel called to work on.

I know. It sounds counterintuitive to do less in order to

get more done. But by trying to do more, we end up with longer lists of things to do, and of course they never get done. It's how we lived in the first half, and by sheer will, we kept up. Sort of. It's time to focus on what matters and just discard the rest.

I'll still find time to watch an occasional action movie, just for some good, noisy fun. Halftime isn't monasticism!

Reflection

1. Make a list of every magazine or newsletter you subscribe to (including your online subscriptions). Do you read all of them regularly? What would happen if you canceled half of them?

2. Has the Internet been a time saver or a time waster for you? What are some ways you could manage this area better?

3. Think back on the last seminar or conference you attended. What did you learn that you could apply to your life and/or business? Did you follow through and change anything as a result?

4. Do you find it difficult to carve out time and space for reflection, prayer, and thinking big thoughts? Why? What do you need to abandon to have more time for these activities?

Wise Companions

The chief malady of man is restless curiosity about things which he cannot understand; and it is not so bad for him to be in error as to be curious to no purpose.

BLAISE PASCAL, *Pensées*

Come now, poor child of man, turn awhile from your business, hide yourself for a little time from restless thoughts, cast away your troublesome cares, put aside your wearisome distractions. Give yourself a little leisure to converse with God, and take your rest awhile in Him.

ANSELM

First things first. Last things not at all.

PETER DRUCKER

CHAPTER 19

Finishing Well
vs. Leaving Well

Not long ago I was invited to lunch by a friend, a businessman I have known for several years. I'll change his name to Doug, though I assure you that both the dialogue and the situation I describe are accurate.

Doug is an interesting man who has spent most of his life in executive roles in big public companies. He has been an A-list candidate for search firms. He has been married more than forty years to the woman he loves. As a very young seventy-year-old, he has no plans to retire. Companies are his mental challenge and his fun. He is now engaged in a partnership with some other businessmen. His role is to mentor the CEOs of twenty companies — different industries, different sizes. He has a small equity stake in several of them.

We spent the early part of the lunch talking about the ways Doug goes about bringing high-quality expertise to these companies through a network of other older business pals who also want to stay engaged but not full-time.

I learned a lot from the conversation that I can apply to the portfolio of nonprofit "companies" I am engaged in — what I call "Bob Inc." My small, expert team and I find great nonprofit entrepreneurs, help them discover what they need, then make sure that's made available. Doug and I are both at the stage where we release and direct energy. We don't supply it. It's a good life.

As our time went on, I sensed that this conversation was prelude to something else. Sure enough. Doug pulled out a copy of something I had written for my semiregular "museletter." He read me a sentence that had gotten him thinking, and then he told me a story of what he had been through recently.

Twice in the preceding two years, Doug had been hospitalized (once for four weeks, the other for six weeks) with a mysterious life-threatening disease. He said the doctors didn't quite know how to attack this lethal disease that had claimed ninety thousand lives in the United States the previous year. In his characteristically straightforward manner, Doug said, "They just put me flat on my back 24/7 in a hospital bed and nuked me intravenously with a cocktail of every antibiotic known to man."

He then asked a question: "What do you think ran through my mind while I was lying alone late at night after the doctor told me I had a fifty-fifty chance of dying?"

"I don't know," I replied. "What was it?"

He leaned into the table and said, "It was all little things. I didn't think at all about the afterlife. I thought,

Am I leaving the way I want to? It was all little things."
He paused a moment to let that sink in; then he said, "And
you know what?"

At a loss for words, I simply asked, "What?"

"It was 90 percent relational. It was not about getting
financial affairs in order, but about getting relationships
in order!

"I know you have written a lot about finishing well.
Have you ever thought about leaving well?"

"Tell me what you mean," I said.

"It is more than religion," he replied. "I'm a believer,
and I have settled that. If you knew you were gonna die
in three weeks, what would you think about? I thought,
How do I die so well that it blesses and encourages people?
How do I die in an other-centered way? I made an in-
ventory of my calling. *What have I left undone?* It was
not so much about contemplation. It was about doing....
What did I need to do? Who would I see? What would
I say? I wanted a PhD in how to die right. I desired the
grace to die well. Dying is another exciting challenge to
do well."

Doug then went on to say he had made a list of the fifty
things he wanted to do before he died. "Forty-five of them
were relational," he said. "It wasn't about *finishing* well
but about *leaving* well."

I don't think any of us likes to thing about "leaving." I
sure don't. But Doug sure got me thinking. Regardless of
how old you are, death is not one of those top-of-the mind

topics to mull over. Yet in reality, any one of us could be gone tomorrow. I love Doug's statement: dying is another exciting challenge to do well.

I'm starting my list.

....

Reflection

1. Do you ever think about dying, or is it something you try to put out of your mind?

2. The Renaissance-era dramatist Ben Johnson once wrote, "The prospect of death wonderfully concentrates the mind." What do you think he meant?

3. My friend Doug calls dying "another exciting challenge to do well." What could be so exciting about dying?

4. If you were to make a list of fifty things to do before you die in order to leave well, what would be on the list?

Wise Companions

Death is not the greatest loss in life. The greatest loss is what dies inside us while we live.

NORMAN COUSINS

Live as if you were to die tomorrow. Learn as if you were to live forever.

MAHATMA GANDHI

Somebody should tell us, right at the start of our lives, that we are dying. Then we might live life to the limit, every minute of every day. Do it! I say. Whatever you want to do, do it now! There are only so many tomorrows.

POPE PAUL VI

"I am the resurrection and the life. Anyone who believes in me will live, even though they die; and whoever lives by believing in me will never die. Do you believe this?"

JOHN 11:25–26

CHAPTER 20

What to Do When You've Made the Wrong Decision

All of us make decisions, particularly the important ones, with incomplete information. And often, when there is no time pressure, we create urgency by our procrastination. We wait for special insight or more facts until the last possible moment. We hope that we can somehow predict the future. We look for certainty in the land of probabilities.

The truth is we can't know the outcomes of our decisions until after we commit. This is not a new issue. Aristotle, the most pragmatic of all the philosophers, spoke of this decision sequence: Know → Understand → Desire → Choose.

Simple but brilliant. Too often people seem to find themselves frozen on the trigger, unable to choose and commit. It's not a new problem.

So, when faced with a go or no-go deadline, you do choose — you *do* pull the trigger. *Then* you get more knowledge, lots more knowledge. In the early 1980s I made what could have been a "bet your company" decision to enter the subscription television business (essentially a one-channel, over-the-air pay TV business) in three big cities: Cincinnati, Chicago, and Minneapolis. In those days Buford Television operated network television stations in small markets like Tyler, Texas, and Fort Smith, Arkansas. My big-time Washington law firm, which represented a network and some other major players, advised me to go for subscription TV. After toiling away for twenty years (quite productively, I might add) in small markets, this was a chance to make a quantum leap into the big leagues. By supplying a movie channel over the air, I could get the jump on cable TV in big cities and make a lot of money in a hurry. In my early forties, I was hot to do just that — to be an instant Ted Turner!

We acquired television licenses in these three cities and scoured the country for more. We put new stations on the air in Cincinnati and Chicago. Just "me and my guys" from Tyler and Fort Smith. Can you imagine! Almost from day one I was haunted by two overpowering emotions: excitement and fear. Excitement in the sense of "This is my big chance to get rich quick." And a deeply felt but certainly unconfessed fear that we small-town boys didn't know what we were doing. We promptly went from zero to eight hundred employees. And, of course, we really didn't know any of these new hires, even the managers. We were spending a fortune on advertising, a call center, and an antenna installation force. Soon enough we discovered that big northern multiethnic metropolitan areas weren't like our comparatively small towns. I felt like Dorothy in *The Wizard of Oz* ("This isn't Kansas, Toto!"). The business took off with early adopters, but we had no idea how permanent these new subscribers were. Sleepless nights ensued. Deep in the pit of my stomach, I knew we were in over our heads.

Uh oh! What do you do when the facts of a decision tell you that you took the wrong road? Two pieces of wisdom were pivotal. One from Oxford don C. S. Lewis, the other from General Electric CEO Jack Welch.

Lewis said, "When you come to a fork in the road and find you have taken the wrong road, don't keep pressing forward trying to prove you were right [a particularly male disease]. You promptly (and painfully) turn back to the fork in the road and embark on the right road" (my paraphrase). I had read that Jack Welch had completely changed the direction of GE (certainly one of the most successful companies of his generation) based on a single question from Peter Drucker: "If you weren't in that line of business today, would you get into it now? If the answer is no, then the decision is clear: get out."

That's just what I did. It was a painful blow to my overheated ego, and it cost my company a million dollars. But it ultimately lost $72 million for the company I sold these stations to. That could have been me. The subscription television business (STV) skyrocketed up then went bust all over the country. Meanwhile, I was free to go on to other, more profitable ventures.

Most of the things that determine the success or failure of an undertaking — whether a business, government, or nonprofit — are beyond our control. Markets rise and decline unpredictably. We constantly misperceive how others will react to what we do. Even with all the data and research in front of us, there is no such thing as a "sure deal."

So what do you do when you have gotten, with the best of intentions, into a relationship, either business or personal, that turns out to be a bad deal, a quagmire, a fiasco? Most of the time, we stubbornly try to ride out the storm. We pray that the tide will turn; we give it second chances, third chances, and even fourth chances. We tough it out for a while, sometimes a long while, because none of us likes to admit defeat. Yet the longer we fail to do what we know is right, the bigger the potential defeat.

If you know that you have made the wrong decision, don't persist forever in a state of denial. Face what my wise friend Jim Collins calls "the brutal facts." And if the facts prove that you're still on the wrong track, bite the bullet, pay the price, and find something better to do.

In other words, get out. When the horse is dead, dismount.

Reflection

1. What is the worst business decision you ever made? How long did it take to resolve the situation? At what cost?

2. Are you currently pursuing a course of action — a new business initiative, an investment, new job — that in your heart you know is the wrong direction for now? What are the "brutal facts" of this situation? What is the right thing to do? What is keeping you from doing the right thing?

3. Some of the greatest figures in business and politics actually had many more failures than successes (e.g., Thomas Edison and Abraham Lincoln). Why is it so difficult to admit our wrong decisions, cut our losses, and get out?

4. The most difficult decisions are often those that require saying no to opportunity or discontinuing a good thing to do something better. Have you ever failed to say no to something and later regretted it? Did anything about your decision-making process change as a result?

Wise Companions

Then he told them many things in parables, saying: "A farmer went out to sow his seed. As he was scattering the seed, some fell along the path, and the birds came and ate it up. Some fell on rocky places, where it did not have much soil. It sprang up quickly, because the soil was shallow. But when the sun came up, the plants were scorched, and they withered because they had no root. Other seed fell among thorns, which grew up and choked the plants. Still other seed fell on good soil, where it produced a crop — a hundred, sixty or thirty times what was sown. Whoever has ears, let them hear."

MATTHEW 13:3–9

The risk of a wrong decision is preferable to the terror of indecision.

MAIMONIDES

A decision is a judgment. It is a choice between alternatives. It is rarely a choice between right and wrong. It is at best a choice between "almost right" and "probably wrong."

PETER DRUCKER

CHAPTER 21

Created for
Our Own Happiness?

For most of us, the first half of our lives might be called a quest for self-sufficiency. We want to carve out our own identities. We want to leave behind us our childhood years and their signs of dependence. My *Merriam-Webster's Dictionary* defines *dependence* as "the quality or state of being influenced or determined by or subject to another." The same dictionary lists no fewer than 219 words beginning with *self* — self-acknowledged, self-authenticating, and self-avowed, just to mention a few. Wow!

Not long ago, I was invited to give a presentation about success to significance to a young secular audience of business leaders and their spouses. I like to watch the body language of such audiences to see how I am being received. The usual range of responses is from polite interest to open encouragement. This time was different.

I had some fans, but about 80 percent of the faces were stony, unreceptive, hostile, and perhaps even threatened by what I was saying. The question almost hung in the air: *Who let this guy in?* Undaunted, I pressed on. I usually do well with affluent audiences because I am one of them, but "slow to warm up" didn't begin to describe this group.

When the question-and-answer time came, a hand shot up from the back. The questioner said, "I'm a believer in the philosophy of Ayn Rand. Her philosophy is based on selfishness, that the best way to live is to look out for yourself. What do you think of that?" Talk about in my face! I mentally recalled from my reading in the 1960s that Rand embodied her philosophy in the character of John Gault who, in the novel *Atlas Shrugged*, found the world of others to be so undesirable that he left to create his own sanctuary in a remote location, a world of independence insulated by his money from the cares and concerns of the world. Not a religious retreat, but a selfish retreat. I babbled something about private property and free will (both of which I am personally grateful for) and quickly went on to the next question.

But afterward this bold assertion of self-sufficiency reverberated around in my consciousness. I clicked on www.aynrand.org (I don't actually suggest you go there) and found the official Ayn Rand explanation: "My philosophy, in essence, is the concept of man as a heroic being, with his own happiness as the moral purpose of his life, with productive achievement as his noblest activity, and reason as his only absolute."

Later I listened to a Teaching Company course (www.teach12.com or 1-800-832-2412) on American literature and heard Professor Arnold Weinstein say that the dominant theme in twentieth-century American literature is "individualism." My view of the questioner softened. Perhaps he was expressing a view that others held but were afraid to speak about in such a forthright and public manner. In fact, it is probably the way most people act in their first-half lives, a predominant "success" worldview. If that's the case, then my speaking of self-transcendence and significance followed by surrender to a higher ideal must have seemed threatening to them, and maybe to you. My wife's review: "They can't imagine what you're talking about. They don't like change. You challenged their way of life."

My host, the man who was responsible for the invitation to speak, called the next day to leave this message: "Your message was perfect for this group. Their evaluation may not reflect it. Actually, it might reflect that they aren't ready for it." Shakespeare famously said, "Readiness is all." This was clearly a first-half group locked on process and precious little else. Would their point of view change as they grew into a different season of life? I wasn't sure as I mused about it.

Reflection

1. To what extent did "the pursuit of happiness" drive your actions in the first half of your life? At what point did that begin to feel unfulfilling? Why?

2. Individualism is not necessarily bad. It has been responsible for much of the innovation and progress in our culture. How do you hold on to the positive qualities of individualism without becoming self-centered and indifferent to others?

3. What are the three values you hold most dear? Have your core values changed from when you were in your twenties, or are they the same? Why?

4. What was happiness to you when you were in your twenties? What is it now?

5. Of those you know personally, who do you admire the most? Least? Why? What qualities in those you admire would you like to emulate?

Wise Companions

Human life, by its very nature, has to be dedicated to something, an enterprise glorious or humble, a destiny illustrious or trivial ... if that life of mine, which only concerns myself, is not directed by me towards something, it will be disjointed, lacking in tension and in "form." In these years, we are witnessing the gigantic spectacle of innumerable human lives wandering about lost in their own labyrinths, through not having anything to which to give themselves.... Given over to itself, every life has been left empty, with nothing to do. And as it has to be filled with something, it invents frivolities for itself ... to false occupations which impose nothing intimate, sincere. Today, it is one thing, tomorrow another, opposite to the first. Life is lost at finding itself all alone. Mere egoism is a labyrinth.

JOSÉ ORTEGA Y GASSET, *The Revolt of the Masses*

Rather, in humility value others above yourselves, not looking to your own interests but each of you to the interests of the others.

PHILIPPIANS 2:3–4

CHAPTER 22

What Are the Odds You Will Be Alive in Ten Years?

When I asked my highly specific wife, Linda, whether she would like to know the day and the hour of her passing, she answered not too seriously, "In my humanness, I'd like to be able to plan. I'd like to clean out my closet."

What about you? What if you knew how long you would live? First of all, would you want to? Would you really want to know how the last chapter of the story of your life plays out? Would you live differently if you knew? What if you had a physical for an insurance policy and were told you had a year to live? Would you rewrite the script for that year?

Well fortunately (that's my point of view), we don't know. The whole thing is an adventure in probabilities. And even the probabilities are shifting sands as new medical information and lifestyle news surfaces. One doctor says to gain weight (my perfectly configured Linda was horrified to hear from her doctor that she should gain nine pounds!). One month later, Ken Cooper, my doctor, tells me (as he does each year), "I want to see less of you next year ... ten pounds less." Sigh.

In any event, the occasion for these particular musings is that this is the day I found that according to a consensus of at least four expert doctors employed by insurance companies in consultation with Dr. Nina Radford, my cardiologist at the Cooper Clinic, I had an 86 percent chance of still being here in ten years. How do they know? Because based on the best modern medical science — every poking, prodding, sticking, and scanning of my aging body that the Cooper Clinic can bring to bear on my heart, lungs, and lower extremities — the "winning" insurance company in this dismal derby is willing to bet real money that there is only a 14 percent chance they will have to pay off on a ten-year term insurance policy. Otherwise, they keep the premium, I continue purring along, and they're home scot-free. And the insurance folks have built in a risk premium for themselves, so the odds might be even a few points better for me.

All of this was occasioned by someone very smart making a major multiyear investment in the work of Leadership Network with only one condition. No board seat. No mandated frequent reports. The money stops only if I die. That's what caused me to look into insurance.

Well, as I said before, these are only probabilities and, fortunately, I don't know. I could live to age ninety-five like my wonderful friend Peter Drucker, who was giving me advice for my next project when I last saw him less than two months before he "graduated" in 2006. Or I could be joining Peter and my son, Ross, tomorrow. The Bible has a lot to say about longevity, but the bottom line is always "We don't know. God does." God trumps medical science. As the title of a book by the strange sage Buckminster Fuller reads, *And It Came to Pass — Not to Stay.*

The year after my son, Ross, died, I almost lost my own life in a plane crash that claimed the lives of four friends (the plane I didn't take). Shortly after the crash, I found myself in the lanai of Peter Drucker's home. I had begun talking of estate planning when Peter abruptly interrupted me. He said, "Bob, I know that you are feeling a sense of your own mortality now, but the truth is you will probably live another thirty years and they will be the best thirty years of your life." I was forty-eight. He was seventy-eight. Here I was looking at someone almost exactly thirty years older than I, someone whose last five years (at that time) had been enormously productive. It was as if he had pulled me gently down to earth again, saying, "Just put one foot in front of the other. Follow your calling. Do what you are supposed to do. Let God take care of the rest." Peter went on to publish fourteen more books and countless articles between that day and his death at age ninety-five.

As for me, I actually felt pretty happy with 86 percent odds for ten more years. I certainly don't intend to retire. I hope I will still be writing a new chapter of "my next book" on my ten-years-from-now birthday, and I hope you will be there to receive it.

Reflection

1. Would you like to know how much longer you have to live, or are you content just to let it happen? Why?

2. If you knew you had exactly ten years to live, what would you do?

3. More than ever before, we have opportunities to extend our lives by having regular physicals, changing our diets and exercise habits, and so on. When was your last physical? What changes have you made in your lifestyle to increase your odds of a longer and more active, dynamic life?

4. For each of the following categories, list everything you want to make sure is not left "undone" before you die: personal/family, professional, spiritual.

Wise Companions

You have searched me, LORD,
 and you know me.
You know when I sit and when I rise;
 you perceive my thoughts from afar.
You discern my going out and my lying down;
 you are familiar with all my ways.
Before a word is on my tongue
 you, LORD, know it completely.

My frame was not hidden from you
 when I was made in the secret place.
When I was woven together in the depths of the earth,
 your eyes saw my unformed body.
All the days ordained for me
 were written in your book
 before one of them came to be.

PSALM 139:1–4, 15–16

CHAPTER 23

The Unsurpassed Joy
of a Shared Dream

It had been an intense month for me, albeit softened by the stimulating climate and environment of Aspen. I was working on a new book that might or might not work. Even during a month to get away from the noisiness of life, there is always a serious stack of email printouts that need answers and a lot of people coming and going. But I mixed this activity with late afternoon walks by the Roaring Fork River, attended some Sunday afternoon concerts, and caught up on last year's movies via DVDs in the evening. I wasn't complaining.

One Saturday I found myself on the back deck of the house we lease each year, breathing Aspen's designer air and reading and relaxing. The piece before me was by David Brooks, my favorite columnist. Here is how it began:

> Douglas Hofstadter was a happily married man. After dinner parties, his wife Carol and he would wash the dishes together and relive the highlights of the conversation they'd just enjoyed. But then, when Carol

was 42 and their children were 5 and 2, Carol died of a brain tumor.

A few months later, Hofstadter was looking at a picture of Carol. He describes what he felt in his recent book, *I Am A Strange Loop*:

> I looked at her face and looked so deeply that I felt I was behind her eyes, and all at once I found myself saying, as tears flowed, "That's me. That's me!"
>
> And those simple words brought back many thoughts that I had had before, about the fusion of our souls into one higher-level entity, about the fact that at the core of both our souls lay our identical hopes and dreams for our children, about the notion that those hopes were not separate or distinct hopes but were just one hope, one clear thing that defined us both, that welded us into a unit, the kind of unit I had but dimly imagined before being married and having children. I realized that though Carol had died, that core piece of her had not died at all, but that it had lived on very determinedly in my brain.
> (*New York Times*, July 20, 2007)

I instantly realized how very alone I was before I married Linda, so alive and available in the house behind me that cool Saturday morning. What a priceless gift it is to share even a moment of life. That's why we look around when we laugh at a good joke — we look to see that others "get it." We have a fleeting moment of shared intimacy.

Think how much more it is to share a dream with another that takes years to unfold, a dream that is filled with moments of shared celebration and, at the other end of the continuum, heartbreak and disappointment. Linda and I have always been utterly together in the flow of life, its ups and downs as the melody of it rises and falls like Beethoven's Fifth Symphony — sometimes stormy, sometimes placid.

There have been times when I have felt alone in the work that now consumes my time, talent, and treasure. I'd be the first to say that this feeling is irrational, baseless in fact. The work that I do is always a shared enterprise. But I am sometimes confronted with a loneliness when someone asks, "What is it that you do?" I attempt to describe my unconventional behavior and their eyes glaze over. I feel like an alien. I sometimes feel that way at Aspen Institute seminars. I always feel that way when I go to meetings of a board I, for some inexplicable reason, serve on at the Kennedy School at Harvard. It's kind of a "Who let that guy into our club?" sensation. I once remarked to Tiziana Dearing, the executive director of that center, "I always feel like I am marginal in those meetings." She said, "Well, you are!" A truth well told. I didn't take it as unkind. Just objective and dispassionate.

Peter Drucker told me when we spent a few moments together in a Washington, D.C., hotel the afternoon before he received the Presidential Medal of Freedom, "You know people like you and me, who think for themselves, are lonely people." That phrase has haunted me ever since. Lonely in a crowd, really.

Then thank God for all those priceless moments when I have had a "Partnership of Minds" (the title of the David Brooks op-ed that got me on this line of thought) with a team of others — a mind merger in common cause, a joy of shared understanding and purpose. Several weeks ago I spent three days with a group of sixty people from all over the country who are guiding others across the success to significance frontier called halftime.

Each person described his personal experience of life in the second half with phrases like the following:

> "I'm in transition."
> "It's a loss of identity and competency."
> "My four children, who seemed so young, are all gone off to college. It's so quiet in our empty nest."
> "I'm not quite sure what comes next."

I wrote down at the top of my page of notes, "We're all pioneers in a new world here."

In the glorious climate that is Aspen in the summer, we hiked, shared meals together, and were moment by moment of a similar mind. We all "got it" almost wordlessly. This group was a heart meld, the kind of transcendent experience that Douglas Hofstadter was carried away with as he looked at his wife's picture: a communication of the spirit, not of the mind; something that could be understood but not explained objectively; a thing to be experienced, not explained.

Further on, Brooks's column continued this way:

Carol's death (for Hofstadter) brought home that when people communicate, they send out little flares into each other's brains. Friends and lovers create feedback loops of ideas and habits and ways of seeing the world. Even though Carol was dead, her habits and perceptions were still active in the minds of those who knew her.

Carol's self was still present, Hofstadter sensed, even though it was fading with time. A self, he believes, is a point of view, a way of seeing the world. It emerges from the conglomeration of all the flares, loops and perceptions that have been shared and developed with others. Douglas's and Carol's selves overlapped, and that did not stop with her passing.

I felt that way when my son, Ross, passed on to another world. And I felt that way in Aspen. Although I eventually returned to the summer heat of Texas, those conversations and, even more, the common spirit Linda and I shared those few days with those noble people will not stop with their passing.

Reflection

1. Successful people often report feeling lonely, marginalized. Do you ever have times when you are with a group of people and you feel completely disconnected, perhaps misunderstood? What do you think causes that?

2. What is it about others that draws you to them? What is it about you that draws others to you? What do you think causes these "connections"?

3. Make a list of those with whom you have a "partnership of the mind." People with whom you can communicate even without saying a word. How would you describe those relationships?

4. Aside from your spouse, how often do you create opportunities to spend time with those with whom you have a deep connection — a partnership of the mind?

Wise Companions

When we honestly ask ourselves which person in our lives means the most to us, we often find that it is those who, instead of giving much advice, solutions, or cures, have chosen rather to share our pain and touch our wounds with a gentle and tender hand. The friend who can be silent with us in a moment of despair or confusion, who can stay with us in an hour of grief and bereavement, who can tolerate not knowing, not curing, not healing and face with us the reality of our powerlessness, that is a friend who cares.

HENRI NOUWEN[16]

When a friend calls to me from the road
And slows his horse to a meaning walk,
I don't stand still and look around
On all the hills I haven't hoed,
And shout from where I am, What is it?
No, not as there is a time to talk.
I thrust my hoe in the mellow ground,
Blade-end up and five feet tall,
And plod: I go up to the stone wall
For a friendly visit.

ROBERT FROST, "A Time to Talk"

CHAPTER 24

Blindsided!

During the tragic wildfires in Southern California in 2007, my friends Ken and Margie Blanchard found themselves with a new situational management problem. Both of them were in Florida — he golfing with college friends, she teaching at a conference — when their son, Scott, left a message on their phone: "Dad, Mom, I don't know where you guys are, but we just had to evacuate our house. It's unbelievable."

Ken's reaction was a combination of spiritual maturity plus just plain right priorities and good character. As he later told me in an email, "I had two immediate reactions. One was that I had been taught as a Christian that God wants us to experience three things from our abundant life: joy, peace, and righteousness. So I held my hand up in a receiving gesture and said, 'I need you, Lord. I want to stay connected to you. I can't go through this without you.' The feeling of joy, peace and righteousness instantly filled my heart again."

Ken's second thought went to a story told by his friend John Ortberg. As a child who frequently lost at Monopoly games with his grandmother, Ortberg recalls his grandmother saying, "John, at the end of the game, it all goes back in the box." Ken realized that, in the end, he couldn't take any of his possessions with him. "What was really important," he said, "was my relationship to my Lord and to people around me. I focused first on the people I love and who love me — my family both at home and at work. Even though San Diego was under siege by uncontrollable fires, everyone in my family came through safe and sound."

The next afternoon Ken got another call from his son, Scott. "Dad, you won't believe it. Our house is standing, but your house is gone." Ken said that he cried with joy. "Scott, that's an answer to Mom's and my prayer. I feel so blessed!" Three eyewitnesses, including a police officer, had reported that Scott's house was gone.

Sometimes life knocks the props out from under you. I'm convinced that none of us reach age fifty without a "rogue wind" of some sort in our lives. Rogue wind is perhaps the most memorable phrase I can recall from countless speech and sermon illustrations I've heard. This week as I was rummaging through a long-ignored drawer looking for something else, I came across a tape of a message by my friend Bill Hybels, the influential pastor of Willow Creek Community Church in Chicago. I first listened to the tape in 1987, the year we lost our only son, Ross, in a drowning accident. Bill is a lifelong sailing enthusiast. He spoke using this powerful metaphor of a sailor's worst fear: a rogue wind that comes without warning out of the blue — completely unexpected, lethal — a monster wind that can smash a sailboat to bits.

Rogue winds happen to everyone. They are unpredictable and unavoidable. Everybody plans a charmed storybook life, but "stuff happens." It's only your reaction that you can control.

A few weeks after Ken's email, I had occasion to talk to Pete Chambers, a thirty-seven-year-old friend and entrepreneur who had received the same kind of call that Ken and Margie had received. At six in the morning on a Friday, an employee called to say that the awards and advertising specialties business he had spent years building was on fire. Pete threw on a pair of shorts, jumped in his car, and was in front of his building within five minutes. A 911 call had the fire department there within five minutes of the fire's discovery. And the fire was breaking news on the local television stations. News helicopters were hovering overhead. There stood Pete thinking, *Everything I worked for might be lost.* He told me, "Under those circumstances you discover what true north is for you. If I didn't know that my identity wasn't invested in that business, I would have been in a fetal position. Sitting in front of the company I owned and had built, I said a flash prayer: 'Okay, God, where are we going with this? What's the plan?' Somehow I believed that something good could come out of even this.

"And it has," said Pete. "The damage was able to be contained by a firewall to just the office part of our operation. The goods weren't damaged. Neither was the computer server with all of our orders and database. A group of dedicated employees performed miracles. We set up shop with laptops and cell phones in a nearby coffee shop, worked all weekend, and were shipping orders by the following Monday. The whole experience drew us closer together. The Bible verse that ran through my mind was the one about all things working together for good. You won't believe it, but I continued to think that throughout the whole experience even though I was upside down."

My wise wife, Linda, who has a way of summarizing events, said, "God has a way of providing what you need." Please, please, don't think this is just wishful thinking and reaction of the moment. In both Ken's and Pete's cases, they responded very similarly to how Linda and I felt in 1987 after we lost Ross — our rogue wind.

A real estate developer friend, Art Ruff, from Dallas who came to visit us in the immediate days after Ross was lost saw how buoyed up I was with adrenaline and prayer, something I have never felt before or since. He had been a captain in the Marine Corps in Vietnam. He said, "I know just how you are feeling. God provided for me during that time in intense firefights when people were dying around me. It was an unbelievable and unreal feeling. I predict that feeling will be there for you as you need it, and then it will fade. You will miss it when it's gone."

Art was right. I do miss those transcendent days, both the agony and joy. But I know it's there 24/7 when I need it. It was then. And it will be again if I'm in pain or distress. It's more real to me than what most people call "reality."

Reflection

1. Have you experienced a "rogue wind"? A misfortune or tragedy that seriously took the wind out of your sails? How did you respond? What did you learn about yourself? About God?

2. My wife says, "God has a way of providing what you need." In your experience, is that wishful thinking, or is it really true? What examples from your own life influenced your answer?

3. Do you depend on God more in times of trial than when things are going well? Why? Is it possible to have the same level of trust in God when things are going well as when they are going badly? Explain.

Wise Companions

"So do not fear, for I am with you; do not be dismayed, for I am your God. I will strengthen you and help you; I will uphold you with my righteous right hand."

ISAIAH 41:10

The unthinking libertine cries that there is no order ... or that God has abandoned human life to the caprices of fate. But perhaps that which seems like confusion to you is really a hidden work of art; and if you could only find that point from which to view things properly, all inequalities would rectify themselves and you would see only wisdom where you saw only disorder before.

JACQUES BENIGNE BOUSSET

Whatever my lot,
Thou hast taught me to say,
It is well,
It is well with my soul.
HORATIO GATES SPAFFORD,
"It Is Well with My Soul,"
written after learning
his family members had
perished in a shipwreck

We can have very little and yet be very rich. A rich soul experiences life differently. It experiences a sense of gratitude for what it has received, rather than resentment for what it hasn't gotten. It faces the future with hope rather than anxiety.

JOHN ORTBERG, *When the Game Is Over,*
It All Goes Back in the Box

CHAPTER 25

That Painting in the Bedroom

Linda and I became collectors of contemporary art in our early married days. We have almost exactly similar tastes and make time to go to museums wherever we travel. It's uncanny how, when entering a gallery of great paintings, we have the same favorites.

In the process of renewing our home owners' insurance this past summer, our agent said his carrier had requested that we get a current appraisal on a large painting by abstract expressionist painter Joan Mitchell. We purchased this picture twenty-six years ago at a New York gallery and thought it was both beautiful and quite expensive at the time. So at our insurance agent's bidding, we photographed the picture and one other by the same artist, and sent them to Sotheby's, a leading art auction firm. Their appraisal came back at fifty times what we paid for those two pictures in 1981. No kidding — 50X! We were stunned.

I use the guest bedroom, where the Mitchells hang, as a sort of reading room, so I have sat directly across from the largest of these two pictures for years, never tiring of the artist's active brush strokes — vibrant yellows and blues to capture the spirit of the bright, sunny landscapes of the south of France, where the American Mitchell lived and worked for the last years of her life. But now I noticed that the painting, being so valuable, began to bother me. For the first time, I began to think of things like how light and humidity might affect the monetary value of this vastly inflated work of art, which was valued at more, much more, than the first house Linda and I lived in.

It may seem odd, but the two paintings now, through no fault of their own, were no longer decoration but money — a lot of money. So one night over dinner I made the following proposal to Linda: "Let's give the paintings to your donor-advised charitable fund at Communities Foundation of Texas, let them send both pictures to the Sotheby's Contemporary Art Auction in November, and you can invest the proceeds in the philanthropy causes you care about." Linda said, "Sounds good to me. We've never been to a Sotheby's auction. It might be fun to go be in the room to see what happens."

And so just before Thanksgiving, that's what we did. It was a thrill. Both of us were as nervous as cats. The pictures had to be sent to Sotheby's in August to be photographed for their extravagant catalog. The largest got a two-page spread. In the meantime, the price of oil had risen to nearly a hundred dollars a barrel. The stock markets were fluctuating wildly, and Sotheby's stock fell by 28 percent the week before the auction. The New York theaters were closed by strikes. I even talked the Communities Foundation of Texas into lowering the reserve, the minimum acceptable price on both pictures.

We turned up at 10:00 a.m. to get a good seat. No problem. It was a cold rainy day and few people were in the room. Uh oh! Fortunately, our pictures were midway in the auction, and by then not only was the room full but phone calls were coming in from the freshly minted megarich from Asia, Russia, and the Middle East to twenty handsome and handsomely attired Sotheby's specialists who reigned over the room. Prayer didn't seem to be a predominant activity in the venue, but Linda and I certainly were active. When the bidding on our large Mitchell began, I looked sideways at Linda. A kaleidoscope of emotions was obvious. She covered her eyes and said, "I can't breathe!"

We needn't have worried. When our large picture came up, the bidding shot right through our reserve price without a pause for breath by the auctioneer. The final bid for our first picture was *twice* the reserve we had so nervously set. The whole thing took about two minutes from the first bid to the hammer falling. Linda had tears in her eyes. Pure joy.

Minutes later the second Mitchell sold for two and a half times our reserve. At least seventy-five records were broken in two weeks of auctions, and more than 258 works sold for $1 million or more. An Andy Warhol portrait of Elizabeth Taylor sold for $23.5 million. Actor Hugh Grant had paid $3.5 million for *Liz* in 2001! Whew!

The *Wall Street Journal* coverage of the art auction quoted one well-known art adviser as saying, "Buyers sought out art for its value as a hard asset. The art market seems bulletproof compared to the financial markets." I recalled serving on a panel years earlier with Dallas real estate mogul Ray Nasher, who said no investment he had ever made as much as his art collection. Go figure! It seems almost surreal to me — fifty times appreciation. What a ride!

Now what? That Thanksgiving seemed like a season of new beginnings for Linda and me. She is excited about having a great deal more capacity for supporting nonprofit ventures she cares about. I have an empty wall across the room from me where the Mitchell used to be. It's a season of divestiture, not accumulation, for us, but perhaps we will find the younger, emerging, underrecognized artists to fill our space — just as we did twenty-six years ago.

I share this story for two reasons. First, because it is so absolutely amazing. I had no idea art could appreciate like this. But I also share it to encourage you to consider entering a season of divestiture instead of accumulation. Look around. You might be surprised at how much you have collected over the years that has more value than you could imagine. Why keep it? Let someone else worry about it, and use the money from the sale to support your passion. You will experience pure joy!

Reflection

1. What overvalued, underused assets do you possess that could be turned to use serving others? Real estate? Jewelry? Stocks? Art? Your company? Oil royalties?

2. What joy do you receive from your "underused assets"? What joy could they bring someone else?

3. What in your life is ready for "planned abandonment" so you can create space for a new beginning?

Wise Companions

The best audience for the practice of virtue is the approval of one's own conscience.

CICERO, *Tusculan Disputations*

"Do not store up for yourselves treasures on earth, where moth and rust destroy, and where thieves break in and steal. But store up for yourselves treasures in heaven."

MATTHEW 6:19–20

Notes

1. Peter Drucker, *Managing the Non Profit Organization* (London: Collins, 1992).

2. Roger Lipsey, *Angelic Mistakes: The Art of Thomas Merton* (Boston: Shambhala/New Seeds, 2006).

3. Barack Obama, interviewed on the *Charlie Rose Show* (October 19, 2006).

4. Jim Collins, *Good to Great and the Social Sectors* (New York: HarperCollins, 2005).

5. Czeslaw Milosz, "Late Ripeness," *Second Space* (New York: HarperCollins/Ecco, 2005). Translated by the author and Robert Hass. Copyright © 2004 by Czeslaw Milosz. Translation copyright © 2004 by Robert Hass. Reprinted by permission of HarperCollins Publishers.

6. Charles Handy, *The Age of Paradox* (Boston: Harvard Business School Press, 1995).

7. Henri Nouwen, with Michael Christensen and Rebecca Laird, *Spiritual Direction: Wisdom for the Long Walk of Faith* (San Francisco: HarperSanFrancisco, 2006).

8. James Mulholland, *Praying Like Jesus: The Lord's Prayer in a Culture of Prosperity* (San Francisco: HarperSanFrancisco, 2001).

9. Forbes.com (electronic daily version of *Forbes* magazine), June 6, 2006.

10. *Forbes*, March 9, 2006.

11. Joel Fleishman, *The Foundation* (New York: Public Affairs, 2007).

12. William Damon and Susan Verducci, *Taking Philanthropy Seriously* (Bloomington: Indiana University Press, 2006).

13. Andrew Carnegie, *The Gospel of Wealth* (Kudzu House, 2008).

14. Ken Blanchard, Paul J. Meyer, and Dick Ruhe, *Know Can Do!: Put Your Know-How into Action* (San Francisco: Berrett-Koehler, 2007).

15. Ibid.

16. Henri Nouwen, *Out of Solitude: Three Meditations on the Christian Life* (Notre Dame, Ind.: Ave Maria Press, 2004).

Recommended Resources

Chapter 2: How to Know When You're in Halftime

William Bridges, *Transitions* (Perseus, 1980). The classic source for anyone anticipating a change.

"The Great Game," *Wall Street Journal*, March 14, 2005 (www.wsj.com). The whole story of what Kasparov is doing with the second half of his life.

The Master's Program (www.mastersprogram.org). A strategic life mentoring program for Christian leaders to help them find their kingdom calling in order to maximize their future potential in kingdom leadership.

Pinnacle Forum America (www.pinnacleforum.com). A national network of Christian key influencers operating at the center of society, using their combined cultural capital to strategically engage and transform lives and the culture.

Chapter 3: Defining Moments

My two favorite DVDs of *King Lear* are the ones featuring Lawrence Olivier and Ian Holm, available on Amazon. com or PBS.org.

My go-to resources for Shakespeare are *The Essential Shakespeare Handbook* (DK Publishing, 2004) and *The*

Complete Dictionary of Shakespeare Quotations (New Orchard Editions, 1986).

Chapter 4: The Metrics of Significance

Drucker Foundation Self-Assessment Tool (Wiley, November 1998). I had a hand in designing this process when I was chairman of the Drucker Foundation. It is like talking to Peter Drucker himself. For a list of trained facilitators, see Leader to Leader Institute (www.pfdf.org).

Peter F. Drucker, *Managing the Non-Profit Organization: Principles and Practices* (Collins, 2006). The service, or nonprofit, sector of our society is growing rapidly (with more than 8 million employees and more than 80 million volunteers), creating a major need for guidelines and expert advice on how to manage these organizations effectively. In my opinion, this is the best book ever written on nonprofit management.

Peter F. Drucker, *Ten Principles for Finding Meaning in the Second Half of Life.* You can get a free download of this at www.activeenergy.net.

Matthew 4:1–11, the three temptations of Jesus, which are the three greatest temptations most success-oriented people face.

Chapter 6: Discarding the Past, Moving On!

Charles Swindoll, *Growing Strong in the Seasons of Life* (Zondervan, 1994).

Max Lucado, *Grace for the Moment* (Nelson, 2000)

Chapter 7: Dancing with the Gorilla

F. Scott Fitzgerald, *The Great Gatsby* (Wordsworth Editions, 1999)

Kurt Vonnegut, *God Bless You, Mr. Rosewater* (Dial Press, 1998)

Chapter 8: The Gift of Silence

Roger Lipsey, *Angelic Mistakes: The Art of Thomas Merton* (New Seeds, 2006).

"Dead Leader Running," a CD of a talk by Wayne Cordeiro given to church leaders at the 2006 Willow Creek Association Leadership Summit; available at www.willowcreek .com/wca_prodsb.asp?invtid=PR29407.

Chapter 9: A Balanced Life

Malcolm Gladwell, "The Cellular Church: How Rick Warren's Congregation Grew," *New Yorker*, September 12, 2005. This is an absolutely terrific article. As a knowledgeable friend said, "He gets it." "The Cellular Church" is the definitive article on the megachurch movement — why it grows so fast. In my opinion, Gladwell is in the direct line of Alexis de Tocqueville (nineteenth century) and Peter Drucker (twentieth century) as a social observer. When you read him (*Tipping Point, Blink*), you understand what's going on. He sees with the eyes of a "foreigner," not a native.

www.opportunity.org.au. Check out this website for Opportunity International, whose mission is "to build a community of passionate supporters partnering to solve poverty and empower lives through micro-enterprise development and training."

Chapter 11: Giving for Results

Jim Collins, *Good to Great and the Social Sectors* (self-published by Jim Collins), available at www.Amazon.com. I believe it was the first self-published book ever to appear on the *Wall Street Journal* bestseller list.

Time magazine Persons of the Year issue, January 2, 2006, www.time.com.

Chapter 12: Antidotes to Aging Badly

Philip Roth, *Everyman* (Vintage, 2007).

Gail Sheehy, *Passages: Predictable Crises of Adult Life* (Ballantine, 2006).

Chapter 13: The Paradox of Power

Pat Williams, *The Paradox of Power* (Warner Faith, 2002).

www.halftime.org. The other side of Leadership Network, resourcing those who are making the transition from success to significance (to surrender) and telling their stories to prove that it can be done and is being done. There is also a free halftime Web-based coaching program here.

www.leadnet.org. This website shows all the things we are involved in at Leadership Network and provides many free leadership resources. Our work is to identify the great innovators in American Christianity, to connect them, and to multiply what they are learning through teaching and idea exchange.

Chapter 14: Prayer as a State of Being

Richard Foster, *Prayer: Finding the Heart's True Home* (HarperOne, 2002).

Dallas Willard, *Hearing God* (InterVarsity, 1999).

Philip Yancey, *Prayer* (Zondervan, 2006).

Chapter 15: Born Again and Again—An Easter Reflection

John C. Maxwell, *The Difference Maker* (Thomas Nelson, 2006).

Albert L. Winseman, Donald O. Clifton, and Cutis Liesveld, *Living Your Strengths* (Gallup, 2003).

Chapter 16: Reviewing Grace

Bob Buford, *Finishing Well* (Integrity, 2005). Features interviews with sixty-two people who are making a difference with their lives in halftime.

Lloyd Reeb, *From Success to Significance* (Zondervan, 2005), written for halftimers who are not necessarily wealthy.

www.amazinggracemovie.com. All manner of good stuff: film clips information, support material, study guides, and the like.

www.halftime.org. Lots of stories of right-now heroes taking on all sorts of challenging halftime tasks in their quests to make the transition from success to significance.

Chapter 17: The More You Have, the Harder It Is to Give It Away

Ken Blanchard and S. Truett Cathy, *The Generosity Factor* (Zondervan, 2002).

Andrew Carnegie, *The Gospel of Wealth* (Book Jungle, 2007). A useful condensed version is available from the Trinity Forum at www.ttf.org/index/resources/items/the-gospel-of-wealth/.

William Damon, *Taking Philanthropy Seriously: Beyond Noble Intentions to Responsible Giving* (Indiana University Press, 2006).

Joel Fleishman, *The Foundation: A Great American Secret; How Private Wealth Is Changing the World* (Perseus, 2007).

Chapter 18: Do Less to Get More Done

Ken Blanchard, Paul J. Meyer, and Dick Ruhe, *Know Can Do! Put Your Know-How into Action* (Berrett-Koehler, 2007).

Kevin A. Miller, *Surviving Information Overload* (Zondervan, 2004).

Chapter 20: What to Do When You've Made the Wrong Decision

Peter F. Drucker, *The Effective Executive* (HarperCollins, 1993). In my opinion, the best book ever written on management — see especially his chapter "The Effective Decision."

Peter Drucker, John Hammond, Ralph Keeney, and Harold Raiffa, *Harvard Business Review on Decision Making* (Harvard Business School Press, 2001).

Nassim Nicholas Taleb, *Fooled by Randomness* (Random House, 2005).

Chapter 21: Created for Our Own Happiness?

Douglas LaBier, *Modern Madness: The Hidden Link between Work and Emotional Conflict* (www.backinprint.com, 2000).

John R. O'Neil, *The Paradox of Success: When Winning at Work Means Losing at Life* (McGraw-Hill Business Paperbacks, 2007).

John Marks Templeton and Norman Vincent Peale, *Discovering the Laws of Life* (Continuum, 1994). This beloved book includes two hundred "laws of life" and appeals to all on the spiritual path. Contributors to "Laws" include Ralph Waldo Emerson, Jesus, Wayne Dyer, Benjamin Franklin, Gerald G. Jampolsky, and Eric Butterworth. Endorsements include Robert Schuller and Billy Graham.

Chapter 24: Blindsided!

Harold Kushner, *When Bad Things Happen to Good People* (Anchor 2004).

C. S. Lewis, *A Grief Observed* (Easton, 2002).

John Ortberg, *When the Game Is Over, It All Goes Back in the Box* (Zondervan, 2007).

Chapter 25: That Painting in the Bedroom

John Steinbeck, *The Pearl* (Penguin, 2000).

Fidelity Charitable Gift Fund. An online version of a donor-advised fund (www.charitablegift.org/). Check also with any trusted financial adviser for advice on donor-advised funds.

National Christian Foundation (www.nationalchristian .com). This is an excellent organization that has helped thousands of givers send more than $1.4 billion to more than fifteen thousand charities.

HALF|TIME
I N S T I T U T E™

The University for Your Second Half™

Founded by Bob Buford in 1998, the Halftime Institute provides successful marketplace men and women with teaching, coaching and connections they need to build a life defined by greater joy, Kingdom impact, and balance.

THE UNIVERSITY FOR YOUR SECOND HALF

The Halftime Institute offers a proven process to build on your success as you pursue significance. You and a group of peers begin an all-new chapter of spiritual, personal and professional purpose — maybe within the context of your current career . . . or perhaps not.

The Halftime Institute is a year-long commitment that begins with a Launch Event: an intensive two days designed to dive deep into a systematic process, reflect and dream, and begin to design a roadmap of next steps.

Then, guided by your Halftime coach and surrounded by others who are on this same journey, you will address tough questions, craft a mission, rearrange commitments, and engage with those you love on a whole new level. We help you avoid many common mistakes of midlife transition.

 halftimeinstitute.org or call 855 2ND HALF

ONE ROAD, TWO PROGRAMS
Through two separate, distinctive offerings, the Halftime Institute provides a process proven to be effective and transformative.

THE MEMBERS PROGRAM is two days with like-minded Halftimers, and then a full year rich in coaching and in community with the men and women in your program.

THE FELLOWS PROGRAM is akin to post-graduate study, more involved and by referral. Deeper and highly personal, it combines intensive coaching and community, networking, time with leading figures and thinkers, and engaging opportunities to bring spouses into the journey.

FROM SUCCESS TO SIGNIFICANCE STORIES
"When I talk to someone ready for more than just this (whatever that may be), I tell them about the Halftime Institute and how it helped me get through the fog. It's the most natural next step into the best God has for you and the rest of your life."

GRADUATE, CLASS OF 2013 To see other Halftimer stories, visit
halftimeinstitute.org/stories

UPCOMING EVENTS

If you are ready to take the next step in your journey, the Halftime Institute has cohorts launching monthly all over the United States.

*For the latest information about these programs and all other events, visit **halftimeinstitute.org/events**.*